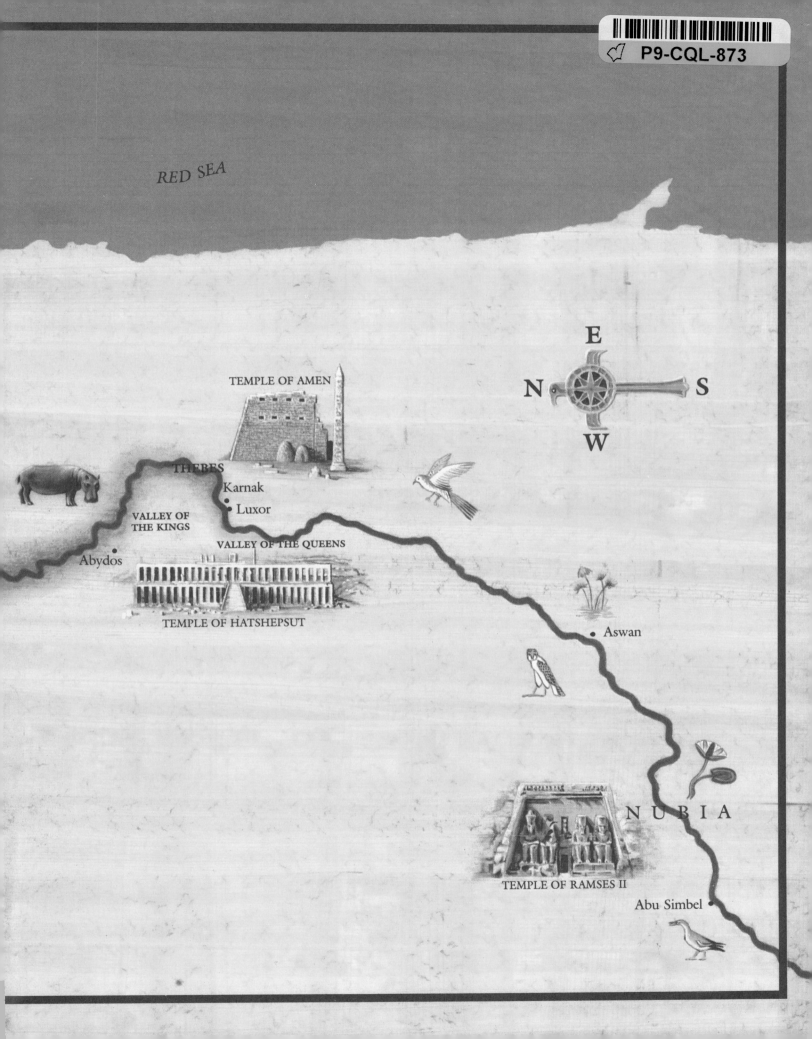

RED SEA

TEMPLE OF AMEN

E

N ⊕ S

W

THEBES

Karnak

Luxor

VALLEY OF
THE KINGS

VALLEY OF THE QUEENS

Abydos

TEMPLE OF HATSHEPSUT

Aswan

N U B I A

TEMPLE OF RAMSES II

Abu Simbel

Cover: The majestic features of an unknown royal figure grace the cedarwood
coffin that once held Ramses the Great.
He was placed in the borrowed coffin
when ancient priests, seeking to protect
his mummy from tomb robbers, removed
the body from its original sarcophagus
and secreted it in an isolated hideaway,
along with the rescued remains of other
pharaohs. The cache was not found until the late 19th century. The sarcophagus
is seen here against a background of ram-
headed sphinxes from Karnak.

End paper: Painted on papyrus by the
artist Paul Breeden, the map shows
the locus of the Egyptian civilization,
the Nile valley. Breeden also painted the
vignettes illustrating the timeline on
pages 158-159.

EGYPT:
LAND OF THE
PHARAOHS

**Library of Congress
Cataloging in Publication Data**
Egypt: Land of the pharaohs / by the editors
of Time-Life Books.
    p. cm.—(Lost civilizations)
    Includes bibliographical references and index.
    ISBN 0-8094-9850-2 (trade)
    ISBN 0-8094-9851-0 (lib. bdg.)
1. Egypt—Antiquities.   2. Excavations
(Archaeology)—Egypt.   3. Egypt—
Civilization—To 332 BC.   I. Time-Life
Books.   II. Series.
DT60.E3 1992   932-dc20   91-36255

LOST CIVILIZATIONS

SERIES EDITOR: Dale M. Brown
Series Administrator: Norma E. Shaw

Editorial staff for *Egypt: Land of the Pharaohs*
Art Director: Susan K. White
Picture Editor: Sally Collins
Text Editors: Charlotte Anker, Kenneth C.
  Danforth, Robert Somerville
Associate Editor/Research: Barbara Sause
Assistant Editor/Research: Constance Contreras
Assistant Art Director: Bill McKenney
Writer: Darcie Conner Johnston
Senior Copy Coordinator: Anne Farr
Picture Coordinator: Gail Feinberg
Editorial Assistant: Patricia D. Whiteford

Special Contributors: Tony Allan, Dale M.
Brown, George Constable, Stephen B. Espie,
Ellen Galford, Susan Perry, Peter Pocock, Dan
Stashower, David S. Thomson (text); Barbara
Fleming, Ira Gitlin, Ellen Gross, Helga Kohl,
Mary Grace Mayberry, Gail Prensky, Sumathi
Raghavan, Valerie Steiker, Bonnie Stutski
(research)

Correspondents: Elisabeth Kraemer-Singh
(Bonn), Christine Hinze (London), Christina
Lieberman (New York), Maria Vincenza
Aloisi (Paris), Ann Natanson (Rome). Valu-
able assistance was also provided by: Barry
Iverson, Nihal Tamraz (Cairo), Elizabeth
Brown (New York), Leonora Dodsworth,
Ann Wise (Rome)

The Consultants:
David O'Connor, professor of Egyptology at
the University of Pennsylvania, digs regularly
at Abydos, ancient cult center of the Egyptian
god Osiris.

Dennis Forbes, a writer and editor specializing
in Egypt, is publisher of *KMT,* a modern
journal of ancient Egypt.

Mark Lehner is a professor of Egyptian archaeology at the Oriental Institute at the University of Chicago. He was the field director
for the study of the Great Sphinx at Giza.

The dates used in this book are often approximate, based on the informed guesses of historians and archaeologists.

EGYPT:
LAND OF THE
PHARAOHS

By the Editors of Time-Life Books

TIME-LIFE BOOKS, ALEXANDRIA, VIRGINIA

CONTENTS

Puncturing morning mists, the Giza pyramids present their timeless profiles to the new day. "They have been contemporaries of lost empires," wrote the French author Théophile Gautier. "They have seen civilizations that we have never known, understood languages that we try to guess through hieroglyphics, known customs that to us seem as fantastical as a dream. They have been there so long that even the stars have changed positions in the sky."

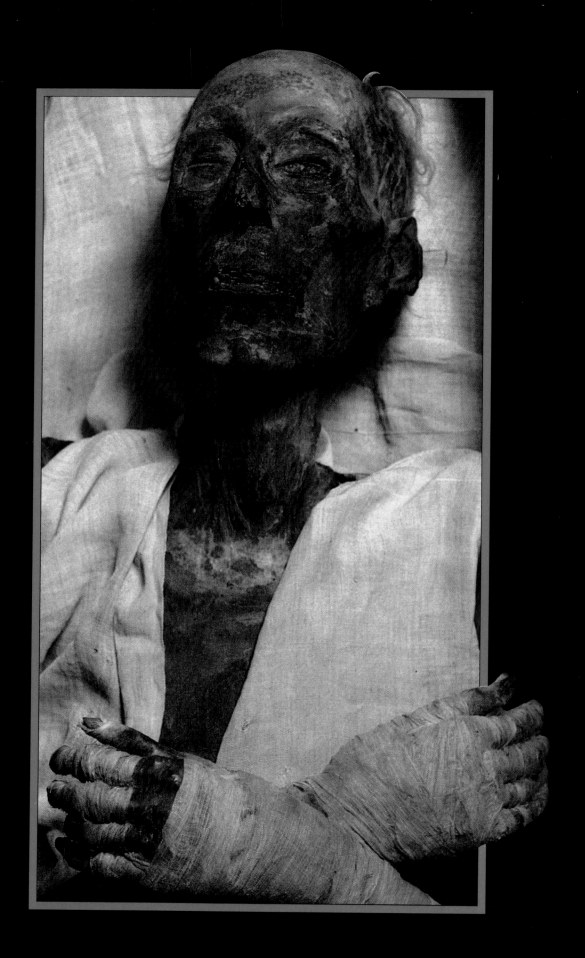

MUMMIES, TOMBS, AND TREASURES

One of the great monuments of ancient Egypt—and one of the most studied—is the 3,400-year-old Luxor Temple, 450 miles up the Nile from Cairo. After decades of intense scrutiny by archaeologists and scholars from around the world, the site seemed to all intents and purposes just about exhausted. The only major challenge remaining was to protect the temple from the inroads of modern civilization. In 1989, inspectors from the Egyptian Antiquities Organization (EAO), alarmed that seepage from Luxor's sewer system and the Nile might be threatening the monument's foundations, arranged for soil samples to be taken to determine the extent of the problem. Workers had dug only a few feet into the temple courtyard when they uncovered a statue lying on its side; soon they had unearthed two more.

The inspectors recognized a momentous find and had the hole filled pending instructions from their Cairo headquarters on how to proceed. The EAO put the director of Luxor antiquities in charge of the excavation, and the digging resumed. The excited workers soon turned up an additional 21 figures—all in excellent condition. Among them was a magnificent eight-foot-tall standing figure. The inscription revealed that the subject was none other than Amenhotep III, the king who had built the temple and had reigned between 1391-1353 BC when Egyptian power, having reached its zenith,

Arms crossed upon its chest in the pose of the Egyptian royal dead, the 3,000-year-old mummy of Ramses II confronts the modern era with the serene impassivity of one who knows eternity.

extended all the way from today's Sudan to modern Iraq.

Examining the king's statue, experts pronounced it one of the most valuable single pieces of sculpture ever to emerge from the soil of Egypt. Some went so far as to say that the discovery of the two dozen masterpieces, dating from Egypt's golden age, equals in archaeological importance the finding of Tutankhamen's tomb 67 years earlier. How the statues came to be buried in the courtyard, no one can say. One theory holds that local priests in the fourth century AD sought to hide them from Romans who had turned the temple precincts into a military encampment. If this is what happened, there may be other items lying buried close by, awaiting discovery.

From the watery marshes of its northern delta to its arid southern reaches, Egypt is a place where, as one contemporary archaeologist has noted, "you can't put your spade in the ground and not find something." This great treasure house of a country has been luring the curious for centuries. Among them have been many who sought to become rich by plundering the past. Others called themselves archaeologists, but by today's stricter standards count as no more than amateurs. The worst of them did more harm than good in their greedy haste to clear a tomb or temple, destroying valuable evidence that might have helped solve many of the riddles still attached to the objects they crated and sent home. But at their best the searchers were magnificent professionals, lovers of history, and great respecters of the humanity behind their finds. They pulled open the doors that stood between present and ancient Egypt, empowering all those who share a fascination with antiquity to step through a kind of magical looking glass into the intriguing land of the pharaohs.

Much of what the world first learned about the Egyptians came from an early obsession with their tombs. Thanks to the dryness that prevails throughout most of the land, not only did these burial sites often contain bodies that had survived the ages largely intact, but with them were found an array of items that revealed much about civilization thousands of years ago. Even when a burial site has been devastated by ancient tomb robbers or modern treasure seekers, it still can tell a great deal. This is something the archaeologist Herbert Eustis Winlock of New York's Metropolitan Museum of Art was to learn in 1920, as he worked on a 4,000-year-old tomb at Deir el Bahri, near the long-vanished city of Thebes.

Shown as they were found in 1920 and then again in contemporary photographs, models of a boat and a granary belonging to an 11th-Dynasty court functionary named Meketre offer a glimpse of daily life in ancient Egypt. Under the boat's canopy sits Meketre himself, while in the granary his estate workers fill bins with wheat as scribes in an adjacent office record the amounts being stored.

Winlock knew that the tomb had been explored twice before, in 1895 and in 1902. But he hoped that his team might uncover some previously overlooked inscriptions that would link two historic kings to the area. His archaeologist's conscience led him to do something his predecessors had not done—draw a plan of the corridors and pits, which meant clearing out the tomb. Although his team found no lost pieces of sculpture—or evidence that might have helped answer the historical questions he had in mind—the seemingly empty corridors gave Winlock, as he put it, "one of the great finds of recent years."

The tomb, which had once held the mummy of an 11th-Dynasty court functionary named Meketre, had long ago been ravaged by robbers and now contained little more than broken stone and rubbish. The clearing operation was almost over when Harry Burton, the photographer who had accompanied the expedition, entered the tomb at sunset to dismiss the workers for the day and found the air "electric with suppressed excitement." One of the workmen had been startled to see chips of stone trickle through a crack between floor and wall. With the overseer, he had begun scraping away other chips piled there, some of which had also slid into the fissure. Burton struck a match in an attempt to light up the cavity; plainly such faint illumination would not do. But so tantalizing was the promise of what might lie hidden in the blackness that he decided to tell others about the opening at once. He dashed off a note to his colleagues, asking them to come to the tomb and bring flashlights.

Winlock, just returned to the main camp from work at another site, greeted the message skeptically. Nevertheless, he and his party went for a look. "There was nothing for us to see," he recalled, "but a ragged hole, but when one by one we lay flat on the ground and shot a beam of light into that crack, one of the most startling sights it is ever a digger's luck to see flashed before us." Winlock found himself "gazing down into the midst of a myriad of brightly painted little men going this way and that."

"A tall, slender girl gazed across at me perfectly composed," he later wrote. "Little men with sticks in their upraised hands drove spotted oxen; rowers tugged at their oars in a fleet of boats, while one ship seemed foundering right in front of me with its bow balanced precariously in the air. And all of this busy going and coming was in uncanny silence, as though the distance back over the forty centuries I looked across was too great for even an echo to reach my ears."

Night was falling, so Winlock and his colleagues could do nothing but plug the crack and wait anxiously for the dawn. The next day they returned to the tomb, taking with them the tools they would need—instruments, drawing boards, reflectors, mirrors. Burton set about taking pictures. He rigged up an ingenious system, using mirrors to beam sunlight from outside the tomb along the full 90 to 100 feet of corridor, where it bounced off reflectors to illuminate the unfolding operation.

The men were concerned that a rush of fresh air into the tiny, roughly hewn chamber, which had been sealed off for 4,000 years, would cause some of the loose stone to separate from the ceiling and crash down on the marvelous figures and boats. Slowly they removed the encumbrances that stood in their way, including a mud-brick wall; to their relief, the ceiling held. At last they had a good look inside. It was not a burial chamber, as they had expected, but "a little secret room" in which the essentials for a happy afterlife had been placed by mourners on behalf of the entombed Meketre.

The Egyptians loved life so much they tried to take it with them to the grave and beyond. In the early days of their long history, they had themselves buried with food and drink. Then they began to add more elaborate appurtenances and comforts to their burial sites, everything from beds and couches to hand mirrors and perfume. As custom evolved, the rich and mighty started taking

A DIET FOR THE LIVING AND THE DEAD

When they died, Egyptians went to the grave with everything they might need in the afterlife—including full-course meals. Edibles—such as the well-preserved bread, duck, dried fish, and figs below found heaped in bowls and on a reed shelf in tombs near Thebes—indicate that the diet of ancient Egypt was remarkably broad and appealing.

Although class determined how varied the fare might be, bread and beer made from wheat and barley were staples for everyone. All Egyptians ate vegetables as well—onions, cucumbers, beans, lentils, peas, and lettuce, to name a few—and such fruits as dates and watermelon. While the poorest peasants may have existed on plant foods only, most Egyptians also consumed a variety of fish and fowl. The wealthy indulged, sometimes to excess, in such luxuries as wine, carefully labeled as to year and vineyard, and in such fatty meats as beef and pork. As a result, some became overweight, with obesity happily dismissed as a sign of prosperity.

Egyptian cooks used oils, thickeners, and spices to concoct their soups and dishes. Among their seasonings were garlic, cumin, coriander, parsley, and fenugreek. Dates, figs, chocolate-like carob, and other fruits sweetened cakes and pastries; honey too served this purpose, but—again—only for those who could afford it.

A mural from the tomb of Nakht, a priest during the reign of Thutmose IV, shows the makings of an opulent feast: grapes; pomegranates; lotus plants, the roots and seeds of which were eaten; cucumbers; eggs; figs; fish; geese; ducks; and pigeons.

so-called servants with them to the tomb—not human beings, but carved figures they believed would care for them in the next world.

Because of his great wealth, Meketre could afford a full assemblage of such tiny helpmates, the largest collection ever uncovered. In 24 little boxes representing rooms and courtyards were cowherds and butchers, bakers and brewers, spinners and weavers, carpenters and scribes—all busily laboring at their assigned tasks. Together they offered an intimate view of what life was like on Meketre's estates. The baker, for example, stood in a vat, kneading the dough with his feet.

The boat models surrounding the boxes represented vessels Meketre would have used for travel and pleasure as he journeyed up and down the Nile visiting his properties. On one of them, Meketre himself sits relaxing, dreamily sniffing a lotus bud; beside him are his young son and a singer, who taps his mouth with his palm to produce a warbling sound. On another of Meketre's vessels, a blind musician plays a harp, anchored in a stand between his knees. Since in reality these narrow boats had to accommodate crews of oarsmen as well as passengers, they would have been too small to hold a kitchen. Thus, even here in the tomb, a floating cook's galley had been provided for the master.

As Winlock examined the models, he noticed several things that puzzled him. A fisherman lacked an arm. Some of the boats bore burn marks or had parts missing, and a few had had their masts wrenched off. Many displayed fly specks; others had been gnawed on by mice that left droppings behind; still others held cobwebs with dead spiders caught in them. Yet, as Winlock knew, there never had been a fire in the little room, and he could find no trace of flies, mice, or spiders on the floor. How to explain the mystery? He reasoned that Meketre had had his funerary models prepared long before his death and kept them in an unused portion of his house, inhabited only by mice, spiders, and flies. He imagined children sneaking in to play with the boats and figures, and they, he concluded, were the ones who had lost the arm off the fisherman and broken and burned the masts.

Here, in a cramped, low-ceilinged room in which they could not even stand upright, the archaeologists had journeyed back in time, meeting Meketre and his entou-

13

rage face to face. And there was to be another eerie confrontation when they moved the boat models and boxes containing the figures out into the sun. Only Winlock and one colleague had touched the objects in the tomb as they shifted them about to be photographed, and they had taken pains to do so gently, with their hands draped in handkerchiefs. Yet in the blazing light they found the treasures covered with fingerprints—the traces, Winlock recognized with amazement, of "the men who had carried them up to the tomb from the house in Thebes 4,000 years ago and left them there for their long rest."

Winlock's discovery offered a window into the past, a glimpse of ordinary people engaged in the kind of tasks that helped sustain Egypt during its nearly 3,500 years of existence. Not only was Egypt one of the first of the ancient civilizations; it endured the longest. The reason for this has much to do with Egypt's location. A land apart, it lies buffered between two deserts and was thus able to evolve in the nourishing valley of the Nile without outside influence or interference. Like a long papyrus stem, it extended in a green, fertile swath only 2 to 14 miles wide from the first cataract of the Nile at Aswan, north to the broad flower head of the delta 700 miles downriver, where the Nile flows into the Mediterranean through a series of channels. The river's annual flooding brought a gift of dark brown silt to farmers' fields and, on the whole, a regularity to life. Egypt's ancient name, Kemet, the word for "black land," refers to this waterborne beneficence.

Truly a blessed people, the Egyptians—who probably numbered no more than five million at any one time—lived through much of their history under the stewardship of semidivine rulers. So numerous were the kings, or pharaohs, who governed the country that some are remembered today in name only, their monuments and

Pharaoh Seti I and his young son, the Crown Prince Ramses, later to become Ramses the Great, confront their heritage in a wall relief in a temple at Abydos. The carvings include the names of 76 kings—enclosed in ovals known as cartouches—running from the inception of Seti's reign in 1306 BC all the way back to Menes, believed to have founded the First Dynasty in 2920 BC.

edicts having long ago disappeared. When historians talk of Egypt, they do so in terms of royal lines or dynasties *(see timeline, pages 158-159)*. They also speak of kingdoms, long eras of Egyptian greatness, and of less happy intermediate periods when political upheaval or foreign invaders destabilized the country. Final decline set in after Egypt fell to Augustus Caesar in 30 BC and became a province of Rome. Slowly, out of neglect, the relics of the proud civilization were swallowed by the sand. Soon even its spoken language was lost.

For centuries afterward, ancient Egypt remained an all-but-mute culture. Travelers from Greek and Roman days right up to the 19th century were enthralled by the monuments poking up from its endless dunes, yet they could not read the mysterious carved inscriptions and could only wonder at their meaning. The 1798-1799 expedition of Napoleon's army to Egypt unearthed many treasures, chief among them the Rosetta stone, whose parallel bands of inscriptions in hieroglyphs (picture script), demotic (a cursive form of Egyptian writing), and Greek provided the key to the ancient signs.

Once again, the Egyptians could speak, and as the deciphering of their writings gathered momentum, they began to emerge in three dimensions, a vibrant, dynamic people. But their past continued to suffer at the hands of the greedy. The looting of their tombs, temples, and buried cities, which had begun as early as Greek and Roman times, reached a frenzied peak in the 19th century. Any object that dynamite, crowbar, battering ram, or human fingers could wrest free from the abundant ruins was fair game. A brisk trade grew up in antiquities, and several European collections became the richer for it.

One of the outsize figures of this harmful commerce—literally as well as figuratively—was an Italian-born strongman and weight-lifter, Giovanni Battista Belzoni. Standing more than six feet six inches tall, Belzoni was as muscular as he was handsome, and enjoyed a sometime career as the "Patagonian Samson" on the London stage. There he amazed audiences with his ability to hoist a 127-pound iron frame onto his shoulders, stand steady as 12 members of the Sadler's Wells Theatre climbed onto it, and then stride around the boards with his burden, nonchalantly waving two flags.

An interest in hydraulics led Belzoni in 1815 to Egypt, where he tried to sell the country's despotic leader, Mohammed 'Ali, a waterwheel he had invented. Belzoni was convinced it would revo-

UNLOCKING THE SECRETS OF THE HIEROGLYPHS

For centuries, Europeans thought that the hieroglyphs carved onto Egyptian monuments were pictographs, each embodying a mystical or spiritual idea, and could not possibly represent the sounds of the Egyptian language. Only after the Rosetta stone, offering a key to hieroglyphs, was discovered in 1799 did the idea that certain hieroglyphs might be phonetic symbols gain some support.

Of the European scholars who labored to decipher Egyptian, Jean-François Champollion of France was particularly qualified to crack the elusive code. Born in 1790, he displayed from boyhood a genius for languages—and a determination to decipher the hieroglyphs that could open the book on much of Egypt's past. In 1821, after years of feverish study of many Egyptian texts, Champollion

corrected and completed another scholar's phonetic transliteration of a royal name on the Rosetta stone—Ptolemy—providing a springboard to further breakthroughs.

The most spectacular of these occurred on September 14, 1822, while Champollion was working on an inscription from a temple at Abu Simbel. Until then, only names and terms from Egypt's Greek-dominated Late Period had

In 1822, the year this portrait was painted, 31-year-old Jean-François Champollion broke the code of Egyptian hieroglyphs when he deciphered the names of the kings Ramses and Thutmose (above). The first modern Egyptologist and the father of Egyptian linguistics, Champollion pursued a brilliant but short career, terminated by his death at the age of 41.

been deciphered. Yet the Egyptians had been carving hieroglyphs as long ago as 3000 BC. Had the script always been fundamentally phonetic, the Frenchman wondered, or were the sound symbols a late development? When he came across an unfamiliar royal name—known to be royal because the cluster of glyphs had been set off in an oval, or cartouche *(top left)*—he recognized the last two signs as *s-s,* and, on the basis of his earlier work, realized that the one preceding them was likely *ms.* The first was a stylized picture of the sun, and Champollion knew that in Coptic, a language derived from ancient Egyptian, the word for "sun" is *re.* Re-ms-s-s. Could this possibly be the 19th-Dynasty pharaoh Ramses? (The hieroglyphic system omits most vowels.) Champollion moved on to a second cartouche, also containing the *ms* and *s* characters *(bottom left).* Here, the first glyph represented a bird—an ibis—which was sacred to the god Thoth. Boldly guessing that the ibis stood for the god's name, Champollion found himself muttering "Thoth-ms-s"—Thutmose, the name of another great king.

Writing of his discovery, which effectively ended debate over the nature of hieroglyphs, Champollion said: "It is a script that is at once pictorial, symbolic, and phonetic within the same text, the same sentence, I would almost say within the same word."

lutionize Egypt's antiquated system of agriculture—and make him rich. When nothing came of the waterwheel caper, he turned to an endeavor that promised an immediate payoff: the exploitation of the ancient treasures scattered about in the desert sands.

Through a Swiss scholar and linguist, Belzoni had heard of the gigantic granite head of a king called the Young Memnon (in fact, it was a portrait of the great pharaoh Ramses II), regarded by one authority of the day as "certainly the most beautiful and perfect piece of Egyptian sculpture that can be seen throughout the whole country." Measuring nine feet high and almost seven feet wide at the shoulders, the piece weighed well over seven tons. Aware of its importance, a group of Frenchmen had tried to remove the head but could not budge it. Belzoni determined to succeed where they had failed. This, he recognized, would be a great prize for the British Museum. "I found it near the remains of its body and chair," he bragged afterward, "with its face upward, and apparently smiling on me, at the thought of being taken to England."

Using a crudely built cart and a contingent of local laborers, Belzoni managed after several days of hauling to get the sculpture to the bank of the Nile. Weeks would elapse before it could be hoisted onto a ship and transported to Cairo and eventually to England, where it produced a sensation worthy of Belzoni's effort.

Belzoni had become addicted to the hunt. He was a zestful fellow, happily crawling in and out of tombs, sometimes spending the night in them. On occasion he lived with the tomb robbers who inhabited the entrances to the larger of these burial places, even dining with them in less-than-sanitary conditions. Whenever the robbers thought he might stay overnight with them, they would kill a couple of chickens and roast them in a small oven heated with fragments of wooden mummy cases, and, as the guest noted, "sometimes even with the bones and wrappings of the former occupants."

Belzoni had plainly gained the confidence of his hosts; he persuaded them to take him into the deep, rock-cut sepulchers from which they obtained the antiquities they sold. Despite the stifling air and the choking dust that rose from the mummies, Belzoni went about his task with gusto—robbing the bodies of their papyri, illustrated texts of supposedly magical content hidden in the coffins or among the wrappings.

Getting into the tombs was not easy, involving as it did tedious crawling through sand-and-rubble-choked passageways. Remaining there for any length of time in the company of the tomb robbers required a special courage. "In some places," Belzoni wrote, "there is not more than a vacancy of a foot left, which you must contrive to pass through in a creeping posture like a snail, on pointed and keen stones that cut like glass." On one occasion, the strongman found himself "surrounded by bodies, by heaps of mummies in all directions; which, previous to my being accustomed to the sight, impressed me with horror. The blackness of the wall, the faint light given by the candles or torches for want of air, the different objects that surrounded me, seeming to converse with each other, and the Arabs with the candles or torches in their hands, naked and covered with dust, themselves resembling living mummies, absolutely formed a scene that cannot be described."

Yet Belzoni did describe his experiences among the Egyptian dead, in a popular book that spared no gruesome detail. He wrote that he counted himself lucky for lacking a sense of smell, but that as he rummaged among the bodies, breathing in their fetid dust, he "could taste that the mummies were rather unpleasant to swallow." Once, as he sat down on a coffin to rest, the weight of his enormous frame bore down on the body inside and "crushed it like a bandbox." Without anything to hold on to, Belzoni sank "among the broken mummies, with a crash of bones, rags, and wooden cases, which raised such a dust as kept me motionless for a quarter of an hour, waiting till it subsided again." When eventually he got up to leave, he raised more dust, "and every step I took I crushed a mummy in some part or other."

On another occasion, Belzoni found himself squeezing through a 20-foot-long passage not much wider than his own body. "It was choked with mummies," he wrote, "and I could not pass without putting my face in contact with that of some decayed Egyptian; but as the passage inclined downward, my own weight helped me on: However, I could not avoid being covered with bones, legs, arms, and heads rolling from above. Thus I proceeded from one cave to another, all full of mummies piled up in various ways, some standing, some lying, and some on their heads."

Amateur though he was, Belzoni made several important finds in Egypt, including the magnificent tomb of Seti I, father of Ramses II. He was soon joined by other Europeans who threw themselves into the treasure hunt with a passion, as a French scholar said, "so violent that it is inferior to love or ambition only in the

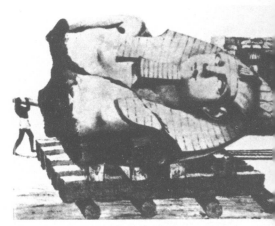

Dapper in 19th-century Egyptian garb, Giovanni Battista Belzoni ran this portrait of himself as the frontispiece to his 1822 book recounting his experiences "within the pyramids, temples, tombs, and excavations" of Egypt. Among his great coups was the recovery of the head of Memnon (actually Ramses II), shown being dragged to the Nile by workmen prior to shipment to England.

pettiness of its aims." The deciphering of hieroglyphs, however, had begun to produce respect among scholars for a past that now seemed in danger of disappearing. The Egyptians themselves, who had long shown little regard for their heritage, rivaled the foreigners in their wanton destruction. Not only did the Egyptians sack ancient sites for items to sell to tourists, but, following an old practice, they quarried monuments to obtain building blocks. (A quarter of the temple at Dendera went into the construction of a saltpeter factory; the temple at Armant surrendered its stones to a sugar-beet refinery.)

It was an interest in Coptic manuscripts that brought Auguste Mariette, a French scholar, to Egypt in 1850. An outgoing man like Belzoni, Mariette soon gave up his literary pursuits in favor of digging. In short order, he gained the support of an influential fellow Frenchman, Ferdinand de Lesseps, who a few years later would mastermind the construction of the Suez Canal. Impressed by Mariette's concern over the fate of Egypt's antiquities, de Lesseps went to the new ruler of the country, Said Pasha, and urged him to appoint his young protégé director of ancient monuments as well as curator of a museum that would be built in Cairo to house new finds. Said Pasha agreed, and at last ancient Egypt had a guardian. Mariette tried to put a halt to the looting and unauthorized excavations. "It behooves us," he wrote, "to preserve Egypt's monuments with care. Five hundred years hence Egypt should still be able to show to the scholars who shall visit her the same monuments that we are now describing."

However lofty his goals, Mariette himself was not above reproach for the archaeological methods he employed. He resorted to dynamite to dislodge what did not come loose easily, and he paid almost no heed to recording the many details of his excavations, something archaeologists today do with obsessive concern for the valuable information that can be garnered from even the smallest scraps of evidence. Mariette cleared more than 300 tombs of their contents at Saqqara, the cemetery of the ancient city of Memphis, and at nearby Giza, site of the Sphinx and the pyramids. Over a lifetime, he dug up 15,000 small antiquities alone and employed as many as 2,780 workers at his digs.

As Mariette and his successors all too quickly learned, there was no easy way to stop the despoiling that had been going on in Egypt since the time of the pharaohs themselves. Rare was the tomb that had not been tunneled into or otherwise entered by robbers, despite all precautions taken by the builders to protect these final resting places. Their futile efforts employed everything from bolts to false passageways, sliding trapdoors of stone, and overhead shafts filled with rubble that came crashing down on anyone trying to dig through such a barrier. Grisly evidence of at least one robber caught at his thievery showed up in a tomb. An archaeologist working there found a pair of severed arms atop a shattered coffin, with the victim's bones lying alongside. The scientist surmised that a robber had been about to lift the mummy from its casket when the tomb's ceiling collapsed, cutting off the arms and at the same time killing him.

An unholy lot, the tomb robbers showed little respect for the dead. One group thought nothing of turning the mummies of children into torches with which to light up their work. In tearing at the wrappings of the pharaohs and their queens in a search for gold, the robbers often ripped off heads, arms, and hands and tossed them aside. They were bold, to say the least. Some apparently worked unhurriedly. One group even had time to set up a little joke, although it would be 3,000 years before anyone else could laugh at it: In a series of burial shafts containing mummified sacred animals, archaeologists came upon a perfectly preserved monkey and dog that had been unwrapped by robbers and propped up beside each other to make it look as though the dog, with its tail curved alertly over its back, were in animated conversation with the monkey.

The robbing of tombs was particularly widespread during hard times, as the evidence provided by court records shows. One document from Thebes tells how "the tombs and sepulchers in which rested the blessed ones of old" had all been broken into by thieves, who pulled the occupants from their coffins and sarcophagi, threw them "out upon the desert," and stole "their articles of household furniture, which had been given them, together with the gold, the silver, and the ornaments which were in their coffins."

One of two wooden coffins in which the mummy of Thutmose I was enclosed bears adz marks left by modern tomb robbers as they hacked off the gold foil that covered much of the carved surface. Apparently as a result of rough handling by ancient thieves who tore at the pharaoh's body for hidden jewels, Thutmose lacked both hands when found in 1881.

Many thieves were caught, and several confessed. "We went to rob the tombs in accordance with our regular habit," one robber told the men who would judge him, "and we found the pyramid of King Sekemre-shedtawy. We took our copper tools and we broke into this pyramid through its innermost part. Then we broke through the rubble and found the pharaoh lying at the back of his burial place. The noble mummy was completely bedecked with gold, and his coffins were adorned with gold and silver inside and out and inlaid with all sorts of precious stones." Beside the king lay his queen, her person similarly adorned.

The thieves collected the items of value belonging to both king and queen and set fire to their coffins, a regular practice among tomb robbers since the fire freed any gold foil still clinging to the wood after most of the precious metal had been stripped off. Then the men divided the gold, jewels, and amulets among themselves and set off for Thebes where, presumably, they disposed of their loot. What punishment this particular fellow received goes unnoted, but the oath taken by another suspect makes chillingly clear the outcome of a guilty verdict: "As Amen lives and as the Ruler lives, if I be found to have had anything to do with any one of the thieves, may I be mutilated in nose and ears and be placed on the stake."

Despite the severity of the punishments meted out by the courts, tomb robbing was so rampant by the 21st Dynasty (1070-945 BC) and the destruction to the royal mummies of the previous three dynasties viewed as so sacrilegious that the priests removed the bodies of the kings and queens from their resting places and assembled them in two well-hidden tombs. In several instances they made repairs to the bodies, reattaching arms and at least one head, that of Seti I *(page 106),* and rewrapping some of the kings before labeling them for identification. Not until the late 19th century were these hiding places found—at Deir el Bahri and in the cliffs of the Valley of the Kings—and then exploited by modern tomb robbers.

The exact details of the discovery of the first cache are somewhat vague and confused, but it appears that in 1871 a goatherd named Ahmed abd er-Rassul went in search of a missing kid, only to find that it had fallen down a deep hole. As he lowered himself into what he realized was in fact a hand-cut shaft, he saw a small doorway carved in the rock. Slipping through it, he entered a veritable Aladdin's cave of antiquities. Ahmed reported his discovery at once to his son and two brothers, and together they began a 10-year-long exploitation of the tomb's treasures. But as the high-quality relics they removed began to appear on the market—a papyrus here, a scarab there, many bearing illustrious names—suspicions about their origins began to grow among the authorities.

When Mariette's successor, Gaston Maspero, heard that pharaonic objects of considerable value were being sold to tourists in Egypt and to collectors in Europe, he knew at once that a spectacular trove had been uncovered and that the plundering had to be stopped if any valuable items were to remain for the Cairo Museum. Pursuing various leads to the thieves' identity, Maspero had Ahmed and one of his brothers arrested. Although the prisoners were beaten on the soles of their feet until their skin hung loose and were subjected to other tortures and humiliations, they refused to divulge their secret.

Ahmed, after his release, now believed that his family owed him something for having endured torture and not revealed the location of the tomb. He was entitled, he said, to half the remaining loot. The eldest surviving sibling, Mohammed, decided the issue by disclosing the source of the family's income to the provincial governor—who informed Emil Brugsch, Maspero's German assistant. For this, Mohammed was made foreman of the Cairo Museum's dig at Thebes and given a reward of 500 pounds, a goodly sum that he generously shared with his brothers. "If he serves the museum with the same skill that he has used for so many years against it," Maspero commented, "we may hope for some magnificent discoveries."

Nothing could have prepared Brugsch for the extraordinary experience that awaited him when Mohammed led him to the cache. Descending the shaft on a rope, Brugsch squeezed through the three-foot-high entrance into a corridor. Immediately he came upon a large whitewashed coffin, bearing the name of a high priest. Beyond lay three more coffins. Then, after lighting a candle in order to see in the darkness, he entered another hallway, strewn with small antiquities. He advanced to a short flight of steps, went down them, and confronted a chamber hollowed from the wall. Here stood more coffins, some of which bulked so large that, as one author has written, they "must have fitted through the tiny doorway of the tomb like corks in a bottle." As he brought the flickering light of his candle to bear on the inscriptions, Brugsch was startled by the names he read—they were a roster of some of Egypt's greatest pharaohs of the New Kingdom, including Seti I, as well as Seti's even more illustrious son,

A hole cut in the wrapped mummy of Thutmose III is the work of robbers who sought the king's heart scarab, an amulet placed in the chest to ensure safe passage to the underworld. Rewrapped in ancient times, the body was stiffened with oars that had been included in the king's tomb to facilitate his journey by solar boat to the next world. The brush may have been used by ancient priests to remove footprints before the tomb was sealed.

Ramses II, "the Great." "I took in the situation with a gasp," reported Brugsch later, "and hurried to the open air lest I should be overcome and the glorious prize, still unrevealed, be lost to science." He feared that the candle he gripped, along with those in the hands of his companions, might ignite the dry, highly flammable wooden coffins, should he or any of the others stumble or faint in the close air.

When he had pulled himself together, Brugsch explored the tomb more fully. At the end of the long corridor he came to a cavernous room, 20 feet long with a 16-foot-high ceiling, where lay the coffins of a Third Intermediate Period priest, Pinedjem II, and his family. Lying all about in the dust were the remnants of their burial goods—flower garlands, shabtis (small funerary figures), vases of bronze, and objects of glass, a precious substance in Egyptian times.

With so rich a trove, Brugsch worried that the locals would learn of the find and come to raid the tomb. He arranged for the contents to be removed quickly, not even bothering to have the coffins and thousands of artifacts photographed in place, which would have contributed greatly to archaeologists' knowledge of the site today. It took 300 workers two days to clear the tomb and as many as a dozen men to lift some of the coffins. The pharaohs, their queens, and their treasures were loaded on a boat for Cairo.

As the vessel drifted out into the river, the Egyptians who had helped empty the tomb watched in silence from the opposite shore. Word had gotten down the Nile about the cargo, and as the boat passed towns along the way, the inhabitants stood along the banks "and made most frantic demonstrations," the women screaming and tearing their hair, the men firing rifles into the air. What Brugsch was witnessing was public mourning, a funeral rite dating back to the time of the pharaohs. The Egyptians were showing the respect due so august a company of the dead, yet perhaps also bemoaning the loss of a treasure that might have made some of them rich.

The arrival of the mummies at Cairo produced a less respectful response from the customs officer, whose duty it was to tax all goods coming into the city. Unable to classify the remains, he wrote them off as *farseekh,* dried fish. In the Cairo Museum the kings were separated from the entourage of 40 bodies and put into display cases of their own, while the lesser figures went into storage.

In time, Maspero organized the unwrapping of the royal mummies, spaced at intervals. The first pharaoh to be examined was Thutmose III. He had received rough treatment earlier at the hands

Dwarfed by the more-than-ten-feet-high sarcophagus of Queen Ahmose Nefertari, Ahmed Kamal wears the satisfied expression of someone who has participated in a magnificent find—the 1881 discovery of 17 mummies of kings and queens of the 17th, 18th, and 19th dynasties. The entrance to the secret cache where they had lain for 2,800 years was only three feet wide, yet somehow the priests who brought the bodies here from their original burial sites managed to squeeze the sarcophagi through the opening.

of Ahmed abd er-Rassul and his brothers, who had cut through the bandages looking for jewels and amulets. When at last Thutmose lay revealed, the once-powerful king, who had led his armies victoriously against his enemies and turned Egypt into a mighty empire, turned out to be in a decrepit state. The pharaoh's head had been torn from his neck and his legs had been ripped from his torso. Remnants of the resin-soaked wrappings still clung to his skin.

Several years elapsed before Maspero had the stomach to try another unwrapping. He chose Ramses II as his subject. Removing layer upon layer of linen bandages, he and his assistants at last confronted the pharaoh, who had lived some 90 years and left Egypt strewn with monuments to his greatness. Maspero was staggered. This king was perfectly preserved, his skin an "earthy brown, splotched with black," his arms crossed on his chest, his face serene, his nose hawkish, slightly bent by the pressure that had been exerted on it by the bandages. The mouth, small yet thick-lipped, contained a black paste, which Maspero partially cut away with scissors to reveal the aged pharaoh's front teeth, still a healthy white.

Maspero and his helpers went on with the unwrapping. They chose next an anonymous mummy that turned out to be that of Queen Ahmose Nefertari. "But," as the archaeologist noted, "the body was no sooner exposed to the outer air than it fell literally into a state of putrefaction, dissolving into black matter which gave out an insupportable smell." Already the more humid air of Cairo was taking its toll of the bodies that had lain inside their dry, airless, and sterile tombs for centuries without decay.

Hoping for better luck, the archaeologists turned to the mummy of Ramses III. First they unwound three layers of bandages, then cut through a canvas casing covered with a thick coat of a cementlike substance. Underneath they found more layers of linen and canvas before reaching a red winding sheet. At last the moment they had been waiting for was at hand. But it proved "a great disappointment, keenly felt by the operators," lamented Maspero. The king's face was covered by a coating of bitumen, which concealed his features.

In time, other mummies from the cache were unwrapped. Amenhotep I lay just as his mourners had left him, garlanded in flowers. As the archaeologists poked among the withered blossoms, they made a startling discovery: An ancient wasp, drawn by the scent, had been trapped in the petals, joining the pharaoh in eternal darkness as the lid was placed on the coffin.

Eugène Lefébure, who had just assumed his duties as director of the French Institute of Archaeology, found himself deeply moved. "Nearly all the mummies," he commented, "were covered with dry garlands and withered lotuses that had lasted intact through the thousands of years, and there was no better way to understand the suspension of time and the halting of decay than to see these immortal flowers on the eternalized bodies." To him it "was the image of an endless sleep."

No mummy reflected this image better than that of Seti I. The king seemed only recently to have taken his last breath, an eyewitness observed, with "a calm and gentle smile" still playing over his lips; from under the lashes of his half-opened eyelids could be seen "an apparently moist and glistening line, the reflection from the white porcelain eyes set into the orbit at the time of burial."

Few are the individuals today who are not stirred or fascinated by the notion of mummies—of human beings who managed to vanquish time. Eons after being embalmed they remain intact, the very embodiment of the Egyptian belief in an afterlife.

The ancient morticians had a godlike role to play in passing the bodies of the pharaohs on to eternity. "O flesh of the king," reads one old lament, "do not decay, do not rot, do not smell unpleasant!" The embalmers, called upon to beat these odds, faced a difficult task, especially in Egypt, where the warm climate hastened decay. In keeping with the gravity of their profession and the holy nature of their subjects—who were seen as being one with Osiris, god of the dead—they sometimes wore masks representing deities, particularly the jackal-headed Anubis, god of embalming, as they went about the more ceremonial aspects of their jobs.

A great deal is known about the mummification process, thanks in part to surviving records, including a long description by the fifth-century-BC Greek historian Herodotus. Early in their history the Egyptians began preserving bodies for posterity. Corpses long buried in the desert remained undecayed years afterward, thanks to dehydration in the hot sand; the uncorrupted bodies must have inspired people to seek such immortality for themselves. But as burials grew more elaborate and came to involve entombment for the rich and powerful, new methods had to be devised to ensure that the flesh

The face of death, this pottery mask—
with eyeholes under the chin—represents
Anubis, protector of the deceased. It was
worn by the chief embalmer, a priest, who
is seen in the wall painting below bend-
ing over a mummified body that has been
laid out on a lion-headed-and-tailed
funerary couch.

The puffed cheeks of the mummy of Queen Nodjmet reveal how embalming techniques could go awry. The embalmers had packed them with a mixture of fat and soda to give the face a more lifelike appearance, but as the mummy dried out, the tightened skin began to crack.

would not decay in the enclosed environment of a burial chamber. Continually improving their techniques, the embalmers raised their craft almost to the level of an art.

There were several methods of preparing a corpse, but the one practiced on the royal dead of the New Kingdom (1550-1070 BC) was the most complicated and the best. Since there was no easy way to keep the internal organs from rotting, they were removed, dried out with salts, treated with oils and liquid resins, and then deposited in special containers known as canopic jars that accompanied the mummy to the grave. (In some later burials the organs were bundled in linen and returned to the body.) More often than not, the brain was extracted from the skull with aid of a long hook passed through the nostrils. The Egyptians put little value on this organ, regarding the heart as the seat of wisdom and feeling, and believing that only it was weighed in the balance at judgment time. Thus the heart was left in the chest cavity, while the rest of the organs were pulled out through an incision made in the abdomen with a flint knife. Once emptied, the cavity was anointed with palm wine and often partially filled with bitumen or resins before being stitched shut. Then the eviscerated body was laid on a bed of natron, a dehydrating salt, and covered with more of the crystals. Originally the salt tended to destroy skin and loosen hair, but later, with further refinements, both were saved.

After losing its fluids to the natron and arid air over a period of 40 days, the desiccated body was washed ceremoniously in Nile water to remove any salt and wrapped in linen strips. Often resins and unguents were added directly to the skin and the bandages themselves as a kind of seal and to create a pleasant odor. In the 21st Dynasty, sand, mud, sawdust, linen, and other substances were inserted under the skin beforehand to flesh out the body, which in drying would shrink. By Ramses III's day, artificial eyeballs were regularly inserted into sockets to restore the curvature of the eyelids; some of these were made of stone, but in at least one case, that of Ramses IV, small onions made a cheap and ready substitute. Great pains were taken to keep the nails from dropping off; fingers and toes were wrapped individually in bandages and, in the case of the pharaohs, often encased in gold sheaths. All told, the mummification process took 70 days.

Throughout, the embalmers were at pains to collect and retain scraps of the body that otherwise might have been discarded; they even kept rags stained with body fluids. Like the internal organs, these were buried near the mummy, in the belief that the dead pharaoh would need every bit of himself in the afterlife. "Your flesh shall rise up for you," runs one ancient text describing the resurrection awaiting the dead, "your bones shall fuse themselves for you, your members shall collect themselves for you, your flesh shall reassemble for you!" As tomb paintings show, the Egyptians imagined the legs twitching back to life, the torso swelling, the soul and the shadow rushing to rejoin the body, and the once-more-alive king turning to worship Re, the sun god, in gratitude for rescuing him from death.

As luck would have it, in 1898, 17 years after the discovery of the cache of royal mummies that so stimulated imaginations, a second spectacular find was made by Victor Loret, who only a short while before had become director of the French Archaeological Service. Loret had been exploring a portion of the Valley of the Kings and had opened and examined one tomb when he happened on another. He climbed inside, his candle lighting the way, and came upon a horrific sight: a body lying on the model of a funeral boat, "all black and hideous," with "its grimacing face turning toward me and looking at me, its long brown hair in sparse bunches around its head." Apparently, robbers had entered the tomb in ancient times, when the oils and resins that had been poured on the mummy were still viscous. In their haste to get at the treasures they had tossed the body aside; it had landed on the boat and stuck fast.

Penetrating deeper into the darkness, Loret and his colleagues entered an immense pillared hall, the decorated burial chamber of Amenhotep II. Toward the back of the room, they spotted the king's sarcophagus. The lid was open, "But was it empty?" Loret anxiously asked himself. He leaned over the edge and could hardly contain his excitement: "Victory! A dark coffin rested in the bottom, having at its head a bunch of flowers and at its feet a wreath of leaves."

Thrilled at the thought of more discoveries to come, Loret

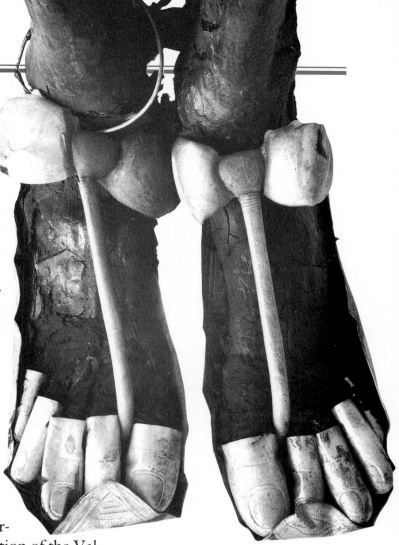

Shod in the golden sandals of a dead pharaoh, the feet of Tutankhamen also wear the gold casings that were placed on each of his toes during the embalming process. The boy-king's feet were in a better state of preservation than much of the rest of his body, the gold having protected them from the oxidation brought about by the unguents with which the mummy had been soaked.

29

moved on, taking pains not to crush any of the valuable objects underfoot. In another room, "An unusually strange sight met our eyes," he wrote. Three unwrapped bodies lay side by side. The first seemed to be female; a thick veil had been draped across her forehead and left eye. One arm had been severed and replaced at her side. She still wore some clothing, although the remnants were torn and ragged. From her well-preserved head, long black curly hair spilled onto the tomb's limestone floor. Her face, in Loret's words, possessed a "majestic gravity." The woman had been laid to rest with her intact arm bent across her chest in a pose that some archaeologists think was reserved for royal female burials. Even in death, she projected a presence, but who might she be? Only in recent years has she been identified as Queen Tiy, mother of Akhenaten, known as the heretic king—and possibly the grandmother of Tutankhamen.

The second body was that of a pubescent boy whose head was shaved except for a single lock of long hair dangling from his temple, the customary haircut for young Egyptian males. The third mummy, a woman—which, because of its bald head, Loret mistook for a man—had half-closed eyes and wore an odd expression, produced by a linen pad inserted between the teeth. Loret likened the appearance to that of a "playful cat with a piece of cloth."

Three more rooms remained to be explored; the entrance of one was closed with limestone blocks, a few of which were missing at the top. Loret hoisted himself up. Though his candle barely shed light on the other side, he could make out nine coffins crowded into a confined space. A couple of days later he climbed over the wall to examine them. Blowing away the dust, he was startled to read the inscriptions—here were the names of Ramses IV, Siptah, Seti II, Thutmose IV, and other equally illustrious pharaohs.

The room itself was too small for the coffins to be opened easily, but Loret was a patient man; he restrained himself from going after the prize right away. In fact, he held off returning to the room until he had cleared the rest of the tomb, a painstaking task involving the removal and cataloging of more than 2,000 objects and fragments. When at last the limestone wall was taken down and the coffins brought out, he approached them calmly—photographing them one at a time, then measuring the mummies within and describing them, before copying all the inscriptions.

Loret was one of a new breed of archaeologist. "Everything was well carried out, foreseen, organized," he could write with pride

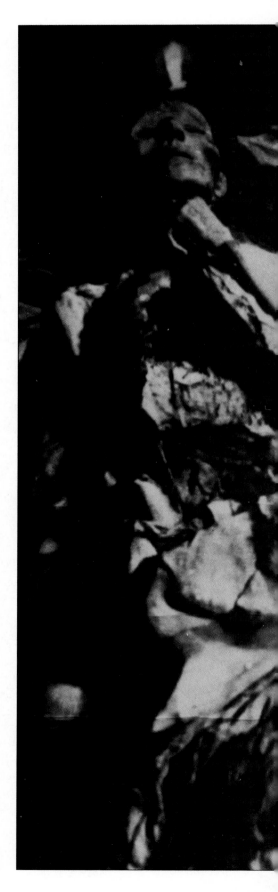

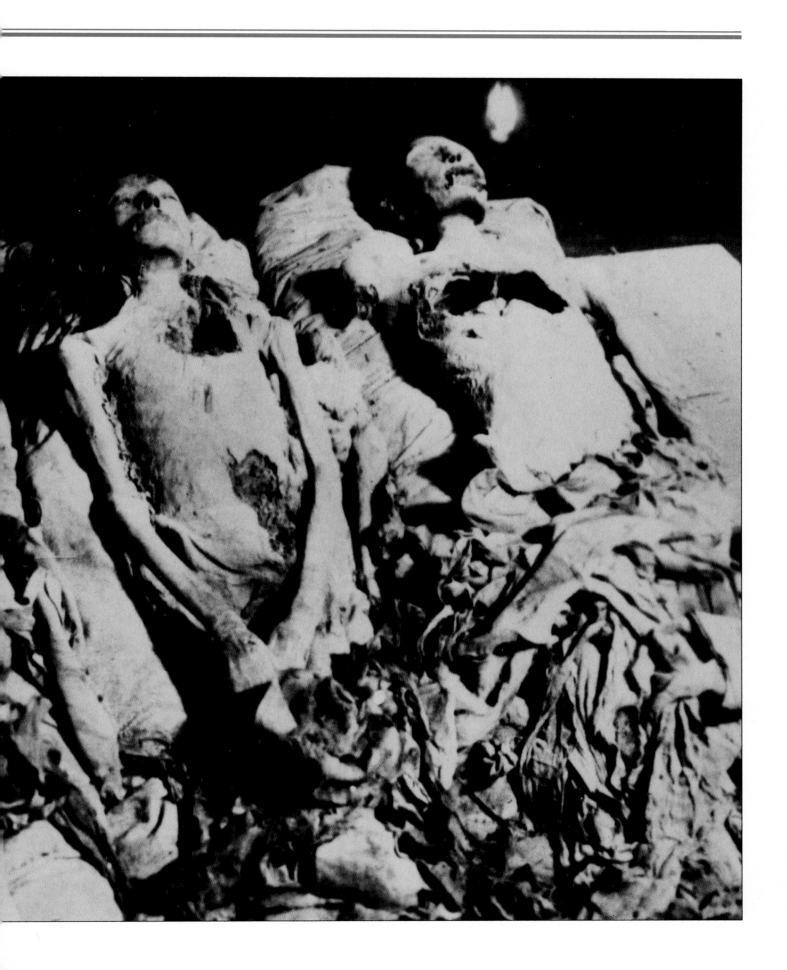

about his work at the tomb. After almost a century of careless exploitation, Egypt's past was at last being treated with respect—and with an eye to future study. At the forefront of this scientific archaeology were two rivals, Flinders Petrie, an Englishman, and George Reisner, an American, both of whom operated in Egypt in the latter part of the 19th century and the early decades of the 20th. They were strong-minded, and though their methods and techniques differed, their goals were alike. They believed that an excavation should be carried out with minute attention to detail, convinced that everything they uncovered had some significance.

Of the two, Reisner was the more compulsive, sinking in the minutiae of his digs until he found it almost impossible to sort through the piles of information and publish readable papers describing his finds. But he became famous for his meticulous excavations around the Giza pyramids, practically his life's work. He won the affection of many and was fondly called Papa George by his admirers and associates.

Petrie, the more colorful, was rough-hewn, bearded, a character with "a constant feverish speed of speech" and a firm belief in the rightness of his own opinions. Passionate about the way an excavation should be conducted, he cared about little else, including his appearance. He thought nothing, for instance, of shedding his clothes during the heat of summer and working in his undershirt and underpants. If these were red, that was all the better because in his view "they kept the tourist at bay" by making him "too queer for inspection!" And he did not mind getting dirty; indeed, he was greatly admired by his workers as the one European who got as dirty as they did on the job. He often took up his abode in tombs and felt no trepidation about sleeping with mummies stored under his bed.

A man of enormous integrity, Petrie did not grow rich from the treasures he unearthed; after the Cairo Museum took its share of the finds, he saw that the remainder were properly distributed to other museums. Lacking wealth, he had to watch his pennies, and the money saved he spent on his excavations. Generally, he allowed himself only a "morning and evening feed" and at night ate directly from cans of food that lined his worktable, even those that had been left open in the heat all day. "Thoughts of digestion must be set aside," commented a visitor as he contemplated the archaeologist's hospitality. Indeed, wrote another, Petrie served "a table so excruciatingly bad that only persons of iron constitution could survive it."

A "WICKED KIND OF DRUGGE"

Mummies were put to strange use in Europe between the 15th and 18th centuries. Ground into powder, they served as the basis of a cure-all that was sprinkled on wounds and even taken internally.

This medicinal fad arose when a black, tarry substance imported from the Near East called *mumia* was seen to benefit patients suffering from a variety of complaints. But when demand for mumia began to outpace supply, a substitute had to be found. Pulverized, resin-soaked mummies produced a similar-looking product that one authority considered "very medicineable," and soon it was being used widely.

Shaking his head over the vogue, the 17th-century doctor and writer, Sir Thomas Browne, was outraged: "Shall we be cured by cannibal mixtures?" he asked. "Surely such diet is dismal vampirism." But no matter how much some railed against it, sales of this "wicked kind of drugge" continued brisk until a story circulated that suppliers were using bodies of the recently dead, rather than those of ancient Egyptians.

Petrie never pulled his punches when evaluating his fellow archaeologists. He openly criticized no less a figure than Mariette for having "most rascally blasted to pieces all the fallen stones of a temple that might better have been lifted by means of a tackle." He railed over "the barbaric sort of regard" that the authorities showed for monuments of the past. "Nothing," he wrote, "seems to be done with any uniform and regular plan, work is begun and left unfinished; no regard is paid to future requirements of exploration. It is sickening to see the rate at which everything is being destroyed." In particular, Petrie could not abide the Abbé Amelineau, a French archaeologist-priest who had worked for five years at the royal tombs of Abydos, a cult center devoted to Osiris, yet had failed to keep any records of where his finds had turned up. It infuriated Petrie that this man could boast "that he had reduced to chips the pieces of stone vases which he did not care to remove, and burnt up the remains of the woodwork of the First Dynasty in his kitchen." He likened such defilers to "the blackbird who used to pick off all the finest bunch of currants, eat one, and leave the rest to rot." And to hammer home his point, he took the thousands of chips that Amelineau had left behind and reassembled them to obtain data about the age of the site.

Petrie spent 45 years digging in Egypt, aided by an uncanny sense of where a discovery might be made. Almost every new season found him at another site, but he was motivated less by a yearning for the big find than by a thirst for information. For him, shards of pottery, mud walls, splintered timbers, corroded weapons, and primitive tools all had a story to tell. He carefully noted where these turned up and in what context, collating his finds and managing each year to publish the results, thus making available to the growing body of Egyptologists the world over all the latest data from the field.

Petrie and Reisner are considered the fathers of the British and American schools of archaeology; their methods revolutionized the profession and influenced people working in countries well beyond Egypt. It was said of Petrie—and the same could be said of Reisner—that "he found archaeology in Egypt a treasure hunt; he left it a science." Indeed, Petrie and Reisner made possible the kind of painstaking detective work that has enabled Egyptologists following in their footsteps to assemble an ever more complete picture of life in ancient Egypt. Thanks to the efforts of such individuals, the Egyptians of old are now better known to us than many other peoples who more lately have come and gone on the world stage.

HOME OF THE GIANTS

Egypt has long cast a spell over those with the good fortune to behold its man-made wonders. Napoleon, about to send his invading army against Egypt's Turkish oppressors, caught sight of the world's most famous monuments on the horizon and declared, "Soldiers! From the summit of yonder pyramids 40 centuries look down upon you." The troops could only have been inspired by the scene as they set out to make history of their own. Although the general's 1798 military expedition ended up a fiasco, a victory of sorts did emerge from the misguided effort—the triumph of the ancient Egyptians over people's imaginations.

The huge team of 167 *savants*—scientists, artists, and other "wise men"—that Napoleon had taken along with his 34,000 troops proved astonishingly successful at their task of making the first systematic studies of the imposing ruins. Out of their efforts came the 24-volume *Description de l'Égypte* that did more than any other work to inflame 19th-century Europeans and Americans with the urge to see, to learn, to penetrate the enigma of this mysterious civilization that had flourished an almost-incomprehensible 4,000 and more years earlier.

Soon all manner of people were invading Egypt: artists, antiquarians, scholars. The famous sites these early visitors saw—most of which had not yet been excavated by archaeologists—looked very different from today. Millennia of shifting sands had half buried the huge pillars and statues. Indeed, some tourists scrambling around the ancient columns carved their names on the capitals, which, thanks to the massive dunes, often lay within easy reach of their penknives.

The paintings and writings of some of the most notable travelers of the day—which serve as the basis for this essay—mirror not just the marvels these intrepid individuals encountered almost every step of the way, but the awe they felt in rediscovering a lost civilization.

Carried away by enthusiasm, English artist David Roberts rearranged the Sphinx and the pyramids in this 1840s lithograph to portray them against a sunset and an advancing sandstorm. Actually, the Sphinx faces east.

*T*hese half-buried pylons, those giant heads rising in ghastly resurrection before the gates of the Temple, were magnificent still. But it was as the splendid prologue to a poem of which only garbled fragments remain. Beyond that entrance lay a smoky, filthy, intricate labyrinth of lanes and passages.

AMELIA B. EDWARDS
A Thousand Miles up the Nile, 1888

This watercolor of the great temple at Luxor by François Charles Cécile, one of Napoleon's savants, shows a minaret rising from a mosque within the monument's precincts, as well as dovecotes and sand partially obscuring the decorated pylons outside. In 1831 the obelisk on the left was removed and shipped to Paris, where it stands today in the Place de la Concorde.

*T*he Colossi don't
look at all colossal; on the
contrary they are quite in keeping
with everything about them, as if they
were the natural size of man,
and we were dwarfs, not they giants.

FLORENCE NIGHTINGALE
Letters from Egypt: A Journey on the Nile, 1849-1850

*The 65-foot-tall Colossi of Memnon,
located opposite Luxor, appear to float
on the annual Nile flood in a lithograph by Roberts. Representing
Amenhotep III, the statues once sat
before the pharaoh's long-vanished
temple. Awe-struck Greek and Roman
travelers regularly inscribed tributes
on the huge monuments.*

The Outer Court of the Temple of Edfou, *painted in 1840 by Roberts, records the pillars still unexcavated, with Egyptians living in the porticoes and conversing in the courtyard. Comparatively young, Edfu was begun in 237 BC and is considered the most beautiful of Egypt's temples.*

The enormous capitals seem to rise from the sand and spread out like a flower without a stem. The temple's proportions put in mind a giant buried up to his waist, overwhelming man's puny stature with his head and shoulders.

JEAN-JACQUES AMPÈRE
Travels in Egypt and Nubia, 1868

*W*e clambered
and slid through the avalanche
of sand, which now separates the two
temples. There they sit, the four
mighty colossi. Before sunrise we were
watching for the first rays. The
day broke; the top of the rock became
golden—the golden rays crept down—
one colossus gave a radiant smile,
as his own glorious sun reached him.

FLORENCE NIGHTINGALE
Letters from Egypt: A Journey on the Nile, 1849-1850

Roberts's 1839 Excavation of Temples
at Abu Simbel *depicts a team of excavators trudging toward the 66-foot-
tall monoliths carved in the cliff above
the Nile. Until it was cleared away,
a vast sandslide blocked entrances to
the two temples built by Ramses II far
up the river as a monument to himself and his favorite wife, Nefertari.*

IN THE SHADOW OF THE PYRAMIDS

One sultry summer's day in 1867, Mark Twain, then a young newspaper reporter, set out from Cairo on a donkey to visit the sandy desert plateau of Giza some five miles to the west, near the ruins of the ancient capital of Memphis. His goal: to climb one of Giza's three famous pyramids and to examine the lion-bodied Sphinx.

Twain's party crossed two arms of the muddy and turbid Nile in a dhow, a small Egyptian boat with a lateen sail, and walked across the desert to the base of the Great Pyramid. The young American felt overpowered by its height; it appeared, he said, "to pierce the skies." With the aid of several muscular Arab guides, and with no small amount of trepidation, he and his colleagues began to climb the pyramid's rough exterior.

When Twain reached the top, 450 feet in the air, he sat down to admire the stunning view. As he later described it in *The Innocents Abroad:* "On the one hand, a mighty sea of yellow sand stretched away toward the ends of the earth, solemn, silent, shorn of vegetation, its solitude uncheered by any forms of creature life. On the other, the Eden of Egypt was spread below us—a broad green floor, cloven by the sinuous river, dotted with villages, its vast distances measured and marked by the diminishing stature of receding clusters of palms. It lay asleep in an enchanted atmosphere. There was

With confident stride, King Djoser of the Third Dynasty—builder of the world's first pyramid—runs a ritual race in a relief carved on the wall of a tiled chamber forming part of his sprawling funerary monument at Saqqara.

no sound, no motion. Away toward the horizon a dozen shapely pyramids watched over ruined Memphis; and at our feet the bland impassable Sphinx looked out upon the picture from her throne in the sands as placidly and pensively as she had looked upon its like full fifty lagging centuries ago."

The expanse of land Mark Twain viewed from atop the Great Pyramid encompasses part of one of the world's most extensive and fascinating strings of archaeological sites. Within this area of Egypt, which stretches from the tiny village of Abu Roash just northwest of Giza to the Faiyum Oasis some 55 miles to the south, archaeologists have uncovered the remains of huge ancient necropolises, or cities of the dead, where the Egyptians laid to rest many of their kings and nobles in large and elaborate tombs. The most famous of these monuments are the pyramids, more than 90 in all, although most are now in such a ruined state that their original shape is barely recognizable. The best-preserved pyramids rise from the sands of Giza and from the nearby necropolises of Saqqara, Dahshur, and Meidum. Ironically, these are also the oldest, built by the pharaohs of the Old Kingdom, a period of about 500 years, from roughly 2575 BC to 2134 BC.

Few monuments of lost civilizations have evoked as much mystery and inspired as much awe as have Egypt's Old Kingdom pyramids. "Man fears time and time fears the pyramids," runs an Arab proverb. They were considered ancient wonders even while pharaohs still ruled over Egypt. By the time of the New Kingdom (1550-1070 BC), Egyptians visited Giza and other sites to pay their respects to long-dead kings and to wonder at the antiquity of the giant tombs. As evidence of their visits, several early Egyptian tourists sketched graffiti on the stone surfaces of the pyramids and their adjacent temples. One tourist, who signed his name "Ahmose, son of Iptah," visited the Step Pyramid of Saqqara about 1600 BC, when it was already a thousand years old, and wrote reverentially that the monument looked "as though heaven were within it." Some 400 years later, another tourist, "Hednakht, son of Tjenro and Tewosret," noted how he had enjoyed a stroll around the Step Pyramid with his brother, and asked the gods to grant him "a full lifetime in serving your good pleasure" and "a goodly burial after a happy old age."

No one in ancient Egypt took more interest in the pyramids and their history than Crown Prince Kaemwaset, the fourth son of Ramses II, one of Egypt's most famous and longest-governing pharaohs. By Ramses's reign (1290-1224 BC), the Old Kingdom pyra-

Designer of King Djoser's Step Pyramid (above, far right), *Imhotep* (left) *is memorialized in bronze. Coming more than 4,000 years after its construction, the English archaeologist Walter Emery—seen here trailed by a chair-bearing helper—would scour the sands of Saqqara, site of the pyramid, searching unsuccessfully for the still-hidden resting place of the architect, whose fame rivals that of his powerful patron.*

mids had existed for 13 centuries. Weathered on the outside by desert winds and sand and ravaged on the inside by tomb robbers, the pyramids and their associated temples had fallen into ruinous neglect. With his father's permission, Prince Kaemwaset set about to restore the pyramids and other Old Kingdom tombs to at least some of their former glory. For these efforts, Kaemwaset is often referred to today as the world's first Egyptologist and archaeologist.

An apparently inquisitive and introspective man who chose priesthood over a military career, Kaemwaset spent long hours, or so later accounts claim, wandering among Old Kingdom ruins at Giza and elsewhere, investigating ancient tombs and temples and puzzling over the writings on their walls. After inspecting a tomb, he would order his workmen to engrave on its face a hieroglyphic inscription that identified the king for whom it was built—creating the forerunner of the modern museum label. Kaemwaset's interest in the past eventually led him to the excavation, as well as the restoration, of several historic sites. He uncovered a variety of artifacts, which he also inscribed with identifying labels. Among his finds was a statue of Kawab, a son of King Khufu, the pharaoh for whom the Great Pyramid at Giza was built. In the inscription he had carved on it, Kaemwaset explained that his work at the old tombs was motivated by his "love for the ancient days" and was undertaken because of "the perfection of all that his ancestors achieved." The prince apparently admired the statue enough to take it home to Memphis, where a fragment of the original was dug up again by the British archaeologist James Edward Quibell in 1908—some 3,200 years later.

The story of the pyramids—and of the necropolises from which they rose—begins in Memphis, the old administrative capital located on the west bank of the Nile, 20 miles upstream from Cairo.

Popular tradition holds that Memphis was founded around 2900 BC by Menes, a powerful chieftain who became Egypt's first king by successfully uniting the many loosely connected agricultural towns and villages along the Nile into a single realm. Its inhabitants originally called the city *Ineb-hedj,* "White Wall"—probably because of the fortresslike whitewashed mud-brick walls that enclosed the king's palace. Memphis eventually became a vast metropolis by ancient standards. The city ran about eight miles from north to south and four miles from east to west, and served as an important political, commercial, and religious center for more than three millennia. From its busy wharves, ships sailed down the Nile to the east coast of the Mediterranean and on to Greece and the Aegean Islands. At the peak of Memphis's power, as many as 50,000 people may have lived and worked there, probably crowded together on narrow streets in two- and three-story mud-brick houses and shops. Many were fine craftsmen, producing a wide variety of goods: furniture with ornate inlays, jewelry made of gold and semiprecious gems, chariots, shields, spears, and other weapons. Most of the people of Memphis, however, worked in nearby fields on the Nile flood plain, raising cattle, sheep, and goats, and cultivating crops of grain and flax.

Memphis remained a prosperous city until the seventh century AD, when the Arabs conquered Egypt and quarried stone from Memphis's buildings to construct the new capital of Cairo. Today, whatever may remain of ancient Memphis lies buried under modern villages and tons of Nile silt, making it difficult and expensive for archaeologists to examine. Only a small portion of the once-great city has been excavated to date, and no traces of its original palace or other early buildings have ever been found.

Almost all of what is known about Old Kingdom life in Memphis—and in Egypt—comes not from the city's living quarters but from its cemeteries. The people of Memphis built their first necropolis on a steep desert escarpment just west of the city. They called it Saqqara, a name derived from that of the Egyptian funerary god, Sokar, and purposely placed it west of their city because they believed another deity, the sun god, Re, started his nightly journey to the underworld from the western skies. Archaeologists have uncovered tombs of nearly all eras of Egyptian history at Saqqara, although most date from the Old Kingdom or before—a period of

Dating back to the Sixth Dynasty, this pleated tunic—one of the earliest pieces of intact clothing ever found—survived the passing millennia in a tomb near Saqqara. The narrow horizontal pleats were folded while the cloth, probably starched, was still wet. A true classic, the tunic's design was popular with Egyptians from the Old Kingdom to the New, a period of 1,500 years.

about 1,000 years, from roughly 3100 BC to 2134 BC. Burials continued at Saqqara until the Christian era, when the necropolis covered an area more than three and a half miles long and almost a mile wide.

The early tombs at Saqqara were rectangular mud-brick structures with flat roofs and slightly sloping sides. Each tomb contained several underground rooms, including a central rock-hewn burial chamber where the body of the deceased rested, together with weapons, toiletry items, and even musical instruments and games. The aboveground portion of the tomb featured smaller storage compartments stocked with food, furniture, tools, wine, and clothing, all the supplies considered necessary for the afterlife of the tomb owner's *ka,* or spirit. Egyptians today call these tombs *mastabas,* an Arabic word meaning "benches," because they resemble, on a much larger scale, the rectangular mud-brick benches still commonly seen outside village homes and shops in Egypt.

As time went on, the mastabas at Saqqara grew larger and more elaborate—up to 12 feet in height, with numerous chambers. It became customary to add a chapel room on the eastern side of the mastaba where relatives of the deceased—or *ka* priests endowed by the deceased's estate—could bring daily offerings of food and drink. On special festival days, the descendants of those buried at Saqqara would gather at the great cemetery to carry out the offering rites themselves and celebrate with a family feast.

Then, around 2630 BC, during the reign of King Djoser of the Third Dynasty, the Saqqara necropolis underwent a profound transformation. By this time the Egyptian kings had gained considerable wealth and absolute authority over their subjects, who considered them in some ways to be living gods. And gods, of course, deserved grand tombs to ensure continuance of their exalted existence in the afterlife. To differentiate his tomb from those of the past, Djoser ordered that it be built of stone rather than of mud bricks, a revolutionary idea at the time. Although stone had lined the floors of several earlier tombs, it had not yet been used to construct an entire Egyptian building.

Djoser placed the design and construction of his tomb in the more-than-capable hands of his vizier, or chief counselor, a brilliant

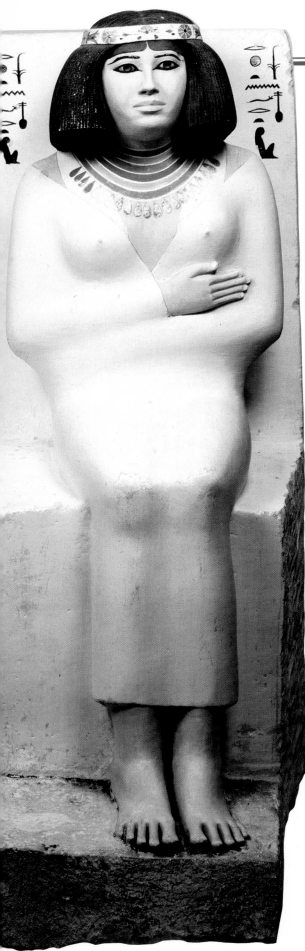

and multitalented man named Imhotep. Changing his mind six different times during the course of the tomb's construction, Imhotep finally settled on a design that resembled six mastabas of diminishing size, one stacked on top of another. The finished monument has become known as the Step Pyramid, a name that may reflect its original spiritual purpose—a staircase for the king to ascend to the heavens after death.

Unparalleled at the time in size or design, the Step Pyramid measured 389 by 462 feet at its base and rose to a height of 204 feet. Yet the pyramid itself made up only part of the massive tomb. Imhotep built a maze of shafts, passageways, galleries, and chambers under the pyramid, and various mortuary buildings, chapels, and courts outside it that were for rituals and ceremonies connected with the king's afterlife. Then Imhotep encircled the entire complex with a huge stone wall, a mile long and 33 feet high, with one true entryway and 13 false ones. The result was a tomb complex truly fit for a god-king.

For this astounding architectural and engineering accomplishment, as well as for his skills as a scribe and wise counselor to the king, Imhotep received the adulation of his countrymen for more than a thousand years and became a minor deity. Temples were raised in his memory centuries after his death, and he became more famous than the king he set out to immortalize. Yet, surprisingly, the Egyptians who revered Imhotep left no clues as to the location of his tomb. During the 1950s, the British archaeologist Walter Emery started a search for the tomb at Saqqara but failed to find it. Emery did uncover the tombs of other noblemen, including one named Hetepka, who held the curious title of "keeper of the diadem and inspector of the king's wigmakers."

Much of what is known today about the Step Pyramid comes from the work of another Egyptologist, a Frenchman, Jean-Philippe Lauer. In 1926, the British archaeologist Cecil Firth hired Lauer, who at 24 was an architecture student in Paris, to assist him with the first systematic excavation of the Step Pyramid. Lauer arrived in Egypt for a short trial period—and stayed for more than 50 years. "As soon as I studied this monument," he told an interviewer in 1991, "I realized its great importance—the first building in the world to be built of cut stone in level courses and designed by Imhotep, the Michelangelo of that epoch. I decided then to devote my life to this work."

Startlingly realistic, these statues—intended to embody the spirits of the sitters, Fourth Dynasty Nofret and her husband Prince Rhahoptep, son of King Snefru—caused workers opening the subjects' tomb to flee at sight of them.

Lauer recalled with special fondness his early days at Saqqara, when he and Firth first explored many of the Step Pyramid's inner chambers. Following passageways planned by Imhotep, the two men slowly worked their way through the huge complex. Lauer remembered the wonder and respect with which he entered one of the chambers, which had been hidden behind a walled door. "We made a hole in this door and Firth, who was rather corpulent, asked me to enter and describe what was inside," he later wrote. "With feelings of great awe, I entered this subterranean gallery which no one had set foot in since it was robbed some 4,000 years ago. I made my way by the light of a candle, and found myself in an oblong room lined with finely dressed and carefully smoothed limestone. It led northward into other rooms closed off with more blocks of dressed stone, some of which were decorated with large stars in low relief."

Although the chambers had been robbed long ago of their treasures, Lauer encountered "one surprise after another" on the walls, including beautifully carved stone reliefs showing King Djoser presiding over religious ceremonies and running a symbolic footrace. Some years later, while exploring the deepest underground galleries of the Step Pyramid complex, Lauer came across the bones of an eight-year-old child and about 40,000 vases, bowls, and dishes made of alabaster, quartz, marble, dolomite, and other valuable stone. The vessels date from before Djoser's reign. Lauer believes that they came from tombs violated by robbers and that Djoser had them placed there out of respect for the dead to whom they once belonged and to restore them to their rightful owners in the afterlife.

Not surprisingly, the kings who immediately succeeded Djoser also wanted giant staircases on which to climb to heaven, and thus ordered their own step pyramids to be built. All of the early efforts at erecting another step pyramid proved unsuccessful, however, due either to faulty construction or to the untimely death of the king for whom the tomb was intended. Not until some 50 years after Djoser's death did the Egyptians finish another large pyramid, an eight-step colossus on the sands of Meidum, a new necropolis located about 40 miles south of Memphis and Saqqara.

The Meidum pyramid would mark a dramatic change in pyramid design, for workmen later packed the tomb's

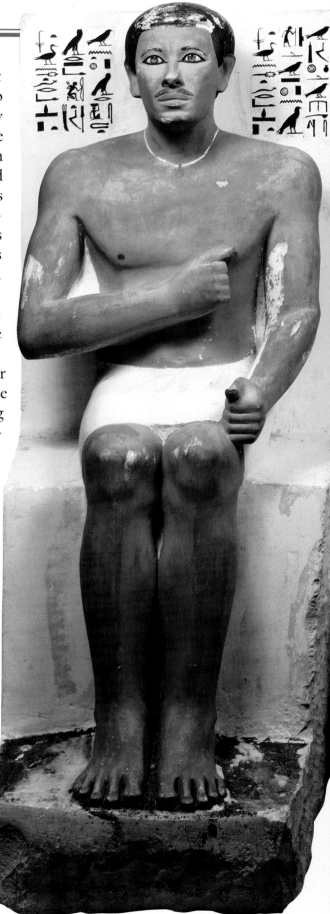

huge steps with rough-cut stones to create a sloping edge, then encased the entire structure with limestone to give it the smooth, continuous sides of a perfect pyramid. Why the Egyptians abandoned the stepped pyramid for a true one is unclear; some scholars believe it had to do with the growing importance of the sun cult in Egypt. Worshipers of Re may have chosen the new design because it emulates the triangular pattern that the sun's rays make when shining down on earth from a break in the clouds. Unfortunately, looters were to make off with the valuable stones from the outer shell, exposing earlier stages of construction. But the huge stone core survived the vandalism, and it towers today strikingly above the rubble that was once its shell.

The Meidum pyramid may have been built for King Huni, the last ruler of the Third Dynasty. Many Egyptologists, however, credit Snefru, the first ruler of the Fourth Dynasty (2575-2551 BC), with ordering the facing of the pyramid—and thus with creating the first true pyramid. Snefru, a king beloved by his subjects and long remembered for his benevolent, gentle disposition, went on to build two more true pyramids—the Bent Pyramid, so named because it angles in to a gentler slope about halfway up, and the Red Pyramid, famous for its reddish limestone. The crooked slope of the Bent Pyramid may reflect the architect's attempt to solve problems caused by an initial gradient that was too steep for the massive blocks of stone—but it may also have made the finished monument seem less than perfect in the eyes of the monarch, especially as his eternal home. Whatever the reason, Snefru abandoned it in favor of the Red Pyramid. He built both pyramids at Dahshur, a necropolis located about halfway between Saqqara and Meidum. Rising to heights of approximately 340 feet, the tombs easily surpassed Djoser's Step Pyramid and became Egypt's largest structures.

But not for long. Snefru's son, Khufu (Cheops), apparently wanting to outdo the massive tombs built by his father, ordered the construction of a pyramid of even greater dimensions at the Giza necropolis, a burial ground north of Memphis with tombs of the nobility dating back to at least the First Dynasty. Khufu was a tyrant, by all accounts as despotic as his father was benevolent. According to legend, he shut down temples during his reign so that his subjects would focus all their efforts on the building of his pyramid.

As work on the monument advanced, either Khufu or his architect changed his mind, shifting the location of the royal burial

A 250-foot-high central core surrounded by rubble is all that remains of the Meidum pyramid, erected around 2600 BC. A precursor of the better-known Giza pyramids, the monument was once sheathed in limestone to give it smooth, sloping sides.

chamber from under the pyramid to deep inside the masonry of the monument. The pyramid's original entrance—which was opened to the public only in 1989—leads down through a sloping passageway to an unfinished chamber, chiseled from the living rock. Abandoning it, workers proceeded to cut a hole in the roof of the tunnel, some 60 feet from the entrance. They then advanced upward through the masonry, cutting away the stone and carving at midpoint a second burial chamber, misnamed in modern times the Queen's Chamber, which they also left incomplete. They then created the 153-foot-long Grand Gallery and a new entrance, as well as the king's actual burial chamber, which they finished in red granite quarried at Aswan, more than 400 miles to the south, and floated downriver to Giza. At its western end Khufu's sarcophagus still stands, although it has long been empty. Why the burial chamber was shifted no one can say with certainty, but some archaeologists have suggested that as the pyramid was being constructed Khufu came to be revered as Re, the sun god. Being buried inside a pyramid would have been appropriate only for Khufu-Re, since Re's symbol, the so-called *ben-ben,* had a conical or pyramidal shape. In the end, Khufu must have been pleased. His tomb, the Great Pyramid, surpassed in size and grandeur any other Egyptian structure before or since. Awed by its dimensions, the ancient Greeks counted the Great Pyramid as one of the Seven Wonders of the World. Its base was immense—756 feet along each side, covering a total of 13.1 acres. As one writer has noted, five major European cathedrals, including Saint Peter's in Rome and Saint Paul's in London, could all be housed within it. The height of the pyramid was equally astounding—482 feet, or 178 feet taller than New York's Statue of Liberty (it has since lost 31 feet of its height to later Egyptians who, over the course of centuries, removed most of its facing for use in building projects).

How did Khufu do it? Some scholars long believed that he used slaves to build the Great Pyramid, which probably took all of his 23-year reign to complete; more likely, he conscripted thousands of peasants for the job and had them work on a rotating basis for periods of several months each, particularly off-season, when the Nile was in flood and the farmers were unable to tend their drowned fields. Working without wheeled vehicles or draft animals and wielding only simple stone and copper tools, the laborers cut, dressed, and transported more than two million limestone blocks, some weighing up to 15 tons, to the building site.

GEORGE REISNER AND THE CASE OF THE MISSING BODY

One of the 20th century's most exciting archaeological discoveries occurred entirely by chance, thanks to a photographer setting up his tripod in front of Khufu's Great Pyramid in 1925. The tripod had nicked out a piece of plaster from a hidden opening cut into the rock. Archaeologists on the scene removed stones and plaster to reveal part of a 100-foot shaft that led to a tomb.

When George Reisner, the American archaeologist who had been working at the pyramids on behalf of Harvard University and the Boston Museum, was alerted to the find, he had all digging stopped until he could arrive from the United States to conduct the excavation himself. On January 26, 1926, he began the job of removing the contents of the tomb. And what a treasure house it proved to be, the earliest virtually intact royal burial ever found, belonging to Queen Hetepheres, mother of Khufu.

The passage of 4,500 years had taken its toll, however. Objects not only lay in a jumble, often where they had collapsed as a result of decay, but also were in such a state of disrepair that to save and remove them all Reisner would need a total of 321 working days.

The most meticulous of archaeologists, he left nothing to chance, resorting to camel's hair brushes and tweezers to dust off and lift the smallest of fragments and stopping frequently to sketch the objects or have them photographed where they lay. In the end, he had 1,701 pages of sketches, plans, and

The archaeologist George Reisner spent more than 40 years excavating on the Giza plateau.

notes and 1,057 photographs to show for his labors, so complete in their details restorers could reconstruct many items from bits and pieces.

But there was a mystery connected with the tomb that even Reisner could not satisfactorily explain. Although the queen's internal organs were in a chest sealed away in a wall—some still immersed in salty embalming fluid—her sarcophagus was empty. Reisner theorized that the queen had originally been buried adjacent to her husband Snefru's own tomb, a pyramid at Dahshur south of Giza, and that robbers had entered her resting place, removed the body for the jewels its wrappings concealed, then abandoned it to the jackals. Unable to tell the king that his mother's body was missing, the supervisor in charge of the royal tombs went through a sham reburial near Khufu's pyramid, filling the new sepulcher with her possessions. Today, several archaeologists dispute Reisner's theory, some saying that if the queen had indeed been reburied, she was more likely shifted from the site excavated by Reisner to one of three pyramid-shaped tombs Khufu erected beside his pyramid.

Queen Hetepheres' furniture, shown in reproduction at the Boston Museum, included a box (foreground) that once held curtains hung from the wooden canopy for privacy.

No one knows just how the Great Pyramid was erected, but the best guess is that a ramp was constructed from the nearby quarry to the site of the monument and that this ramp wound around the pyramid, growing taller as the construction proceeded—thus enabling the laborers to put the stones in place at ever greater heights. But if such a large ramp was used, what was it made of? Some Egyptologists think it was formed of mud bricks—but there are no traces of them in the surrounding area. The more likely material is the debris that today fills the quarry—tons of gypsum, limestone chips, and clay.

Despite the immense weight and unwieldiness of the stones, the workmen positioned the blocks on the monument with such precision that, in many places, nothing thicker than a postcard can be slipped between them. More amazing, perhaps, is the accuracy with which they carried out their task. The pyramid's base forms an almost perfect square, aligned true north, with the northern side veering from the southern by just an inch. The British archaeologist Flinders Petrie, who did some of his early work at the pyramids, was the first to measure them precisely. He was drawn to Egypt by the theories of the Scottish astronomer Charles Piazzi Smyth. Smyth believed that the Great Pyramid reflected divine measures of time as well as distance and also that it revealed the distance from the earth to the sun when its height in inches was multiplied by 10 to the 9th power—10 to 9 being the proportion of height to width of the pyramid. Smyth had argued that the perimeter of the pyramid, reckoned in so-called pyramid inches, equaled 1,000 times 365.2, the number of days in a solar year. To the disappointment of Smyth's supporters, Petrie's measurements proved otherwise.

Only recently did the American Egyptologist Mark Lehner come upon evidence suggesting how the Egyptians might, in fact, have achieved their accuracy. He found a series of evenly spaced sockets cut into the rock on which the pyramid rests that run parallel to the base. Lehner theorizes that the engineers used these sockets to hold stakes, between which they stretched a line for aligning and leveling the base.

The ancient workers seemed to have taken justifiable pride in their pyramid-building skills, sometimes painting or etching boastful nicknames for their particular construction team onto the huge stones with which they struggled—names like the Victorious Gang, the Enduring Gang, and the Craftsman Gang. The teams

In an aerial view, the three pyramids of the Giza plateau rise from the ruins of temples and tombs that once surrounded them. From left to right are the pyramids of Menkaure, Khafre, and Khufu—the Great Pyramid. Seen in the lower right is the Sphinx. The tombs take on different colors throughout the day—silver in the moonlight, gray at dawn, gold at noon, and rose in the sunset.

worked in the sun from dawn to dusk, served by a flurry of porters whose regular deliveries of food and water helped to keep the workers from collapsing.

Egyptologists have long been intrigued by the question of where Khufu housed his army of workmen. Several thousand must have lived in barracks on the Giza plateau. But where? To Lehner it seemed "archaeologically impossible that the traces of thousands of workmen, of their dwellings and their building ramps, their surveyors' marks, could disappear totally."

In 1988, Lehner and Zahi Hawass, director of archaeology at Giza and Saqqara for the Egyptian Antiquities Organization, began a joint excavation in a sandy bowl-like depression south of the Great Pyramid, the most likely site, they believed, for a workers' barracks. A decade earlier, a group of Austrian archaeologists had found pottery, ashes, and fish bones at the same site—tentative clues that it had been an ancient camp of some kind. Within weeks of beginning their dig, Lehner and Hawass uncovered the remains of a combination bakery and brewery dating back to the Fourth Dynasty, a strong indication that the laborers' quarters were not far away. Both men reasoned that it would have been unusual, as Lehner said, "to have a granary and a bakery out in the middle of nowhere."

The two archaeologists also discovered several small tombs positioned haphazardly in the ground—perhaps the gravesites of workers who died building the pyramids. Hawass believes the excavation will eventually uncover two villages under the sands of Giza— one for the artisans who quarried and dressed the stone, the other for the workers who moved them into place.

While much of the building stone for the pyramid was cut from the quarry located right on the Giza plateau, the fine white limestone for casing the pyramid came from Tura across the Nile, and the granite for the king's burial chamber came from Aswan, 400 miles upriver. Just how the pyramid's workers moved the huge stone blocks across land from the Giza quarries and from the Nile harbor has long baffled scholars. Most likely, teams of men, tugging at ropes strung over their shoulders, hauled the stones along the wet ramp, up to the working level of the pyramid. Henri Chevrier, a French architect, tested this theory with 50 men and a one-ton block of limestone set on a track of moist Nile mud. He was amazed to find that the huge stone could easily be moved on a level surface—and by only one man harnessed to the rope, not 50.

DWARFS WHO DELIGHTED HIS MAJESTY

Little people had a special role to play in the courts of ancient Egypt, lifting hearts with their charms and talents. Records reveal how eagerly the boy-king, Neferkare Pepi II (2246-2152 BC), awaited the arrival of a dancing African Pygmy aboard one of his ships returning from Nubia. He fretted lest some mishap befall him. "Hurry and bring with you this Pygmy to delight the heart," he wrote to Harkhuf, commander of his expedition. "When he goes down with you into the ship, get worthy men to be around him on deck, lest he fall into the water."

In addition to providing entertainment for king and court, Pygmies and dwarfs served the priesthood in religious rituals that made

58

use of their dancing and related skills. And dwarfs known as *nmiu* typically attended pharaohs in jobs reserved expressly for them, such as looking after domestic animals, caring for the king's food and clothing, and making jewelry. *Nmiu* were native-born Egyptians, stunted by their genetic inheritance, and differentiated from the *dng,* African Pygmies who, while short in stature, were normally proportioned.

Archaeologists working in Egypt had identified the remains of some 50 dwarfs by 1990, when Zahi Hawass, Director General of the Giza Pyramids and Saqqara, found in a tomb near King Khafre's pyramid on the Giza plateau the skeleton of a dwarf who had been cupbearer to that pharaoh. On the tomb's north side, housed in a mastaba, stood an 18-inch-tall basalt statue of a seated dwarf clutching a staff *(below, left)* and bearing the inscription, "Pyrnyankhu, he who pleases His Majesty every day in the Great Palace."

Hawass called the statue's discovery—in an area that had already been much studied by archaeologists—"the most exciting moment of my life. I lifted it out carefully, like a baby," he remembered. "This is magnificent, I said—our dwarf!"

Examination of Pyrnyankhu's remains show him to have been a hunchback with a large head and very short legs. The tomb of his wife, Nihathorankh, who had risen to become a priestess of the goddess Hathor, was found nearby.

Almost as important as the pyramid itself was the funerary complex around it. Khufu's complex—which deviated in several ways from Djoser's—became the standard for others to come. Here the surrounding wall enclosed the pyramid only. Beyond lay a trio of smaller "satellite" pyramids for the ruler's three queens, as well as several fields of mastaba tombs and two temples, connected to each other and to the main pyramid by a causeway. Today, however, part of the Great Pyramid's original temple complex lies buried under the houses of the suburban Cairo village of Nazlet el Simman. The site contains the remains of the Valley Temple, where priests conducted the initial burial rites for Khufu, and a long section of its causeway, the enclosed ceremonial walkway through which funeral attendants transported Khufu's mummified body from the Valley Temple to the pyramid's burial chamber.

Until recently, archaeologists believed there was little chance of finding and recovering these missing sections of Khufu's pyramid complex, and could only guess at their exact location. Then, in 1990, workmen installing sewerage under the streets of Nazlet el Simman hit upon part of the Valley Temple and a section of the causeway. Hawass called a temporary halt to the laying of the pipes and probed the site. From their brief excavation, the archaeologists were able to determine the original path for the causeway. The Egyptian government eventually hopes to move the residents of Nazlet el Simman to other housing in the Cairo area to allow a complete excavation and restoration of Khufu's Great Pyramid complex.

Back in 1954, a routine clearing away of debris from the southern base of the Great Pyramid had resulted in the spectacular discovery by the Egyptian architect-archaeologist Kamal el Mallakh of another lost part of King Khufu's tomb—burial pits containing sacred boats that were probably used in the king's funeral rites. The first of these vessels was removed and reconstructed in a painstaking process *(pages 61-65)* and is on display today in a special museum beside the pyramid.

Egyptian authorities are concerned, however, that the boat's ancient timbers might not withstand modern air pollution and the extremes of Egyptian temperature and humidity. Thus they have been reluctant to excavate a second boat, which remains sealed in its limestone-topped pit. The craft's presence had only been a guess until 1987, when a team of experts under the direction of the Egyptian Antiquities Organization received permission to take samples of its trapped air. If the pit was hermetically sealed, as the scientists hoped, then its air would be more than four millennia old. It might yield information about the natural environment of ancient Egypt. After long hours of planning and with the aid of highly sophisticated equipment to prevent any outside air from entering the pit, the scientists lowered a stainless-steel tube into the chamber through an air-locked hole. They gathered eight gallons of air, packing it into six canisters for shipment to laboratories in both Egypt and the United States. Later that night, the scientists lowered a camera into the pit to study its contents. As the camera scanned the dismantled parts of the buried boat, its lens suddenly focused on a moving object on top of a piece of wood. "A bug!" cried one of the observers gathered around the video screen set up outside the pit. Any hope that the boat pit contained ancient air vanished.

After Khufu's death, his son Khafre and grandson Menkaure built two additional but smaller pyramids on the Giza plateau, complete with temples, causeways, and subsidiary tombs.

The Egyptians also provided Giza with a permanent guardian: the Great Sphinx. King Khafre ordered the colossal statue, which is 240 feet long and 66 feet high at its head, to be carved from a ragged outcrop left behind at a quarry site by Khufu's workmen. The statue has Khafre's face, complete with his royal headdress and traditional false beard, but the body is that of a reclining lion, the mythical creature the Egyptians believed guarded sacred sites. What, if any, additional significance may have been ascribed to the Great Sphinx by its makers remains a mystery. Lehner, the American Egyptologist, has proposed that the Great Sphinx is Khafre transformed into Horus, the Egyptian god of kingship, presenting offerings to Re, the sun god. In substantiation of his theory, he points out that the Egyptians completed their transition to a solar-oriented religion around the time of Khafre's reign.

Although the Sphinx has been cleared down to bedrock since 1926, for most of its 4,500 years it has crouched buried up to its neck under huge drifts of sand. Through the centuries, several attempts had been made to clear the sand away. Thutmose IV, son of Amenhotep II, undertook the first and most dramatic of these uncoverings that scholars know of around 1400 BC—and all because of a dream he had while napping one afternoon on the Giza plateau. Thutmose

THE BOAT THAT JOURNEYED THROUGH TIME

In the spring of 1954, during a routine clearing of rubble from the southern base of the Great Pyramid at Giza, a rare find came to light. Workmen at first uncovered what appeared to be part of the pyramid's enclosure wall. But the Egyptian archaeologist Kamal el Mallakh noticed that this section was much closer to the pyramid than others on the north and west sides. Suspecting that the wall had been placed to hide something, he instructed the laborers to dig deeper. They soon exposed a row of 81 huge limestone blocks in separate sets, apparently covering twin pits.

A few days later, Mallakh opened a small hole in one of the six-foot-thick slabs. After clearing away the fragments, he peered through the hole. Because of the darkness he saw nothing. "Like a cat, I closed my eyes," he later recalled. "And then with my eyes closed, I smelled incense, a very holy, holy, holy smell. I smelt time. I smelt centuries. I smelt history."

Peering down into the cavity with the aid of sunlight reflected off his shaving mirror, Mallakh made out the pointed tip of an oar and realized that he had indeed come upon an astounding historical relic. Only a few feet beneath him lay the disassembled pieces of an entire cedar boat—part of the funeral trove for Khufu, builder of the Great Pyramid, who had died nearly 4,500 years before.

One of the few surviving large artifacts to have belonged to the Old Kingdom ruler, the boat was remarkably well preserved—a tribute to the care with which the ancient Egyptians had sealed it in its pit.

As detailed on the following pages, archaeologists were no less cautious, taking 16 years to remove and rebuild the craft. Not wishing to press their luck, they have left a second vessel in the adjoining pit untouched.

Workers carefully hoist a hull section of the world's oldest boat from the 12-foot-deep pit in which it lay for 4,500 years. The last pieces were removed three years after the initial discovery.

AN EGYPTIAN RESTORER
TURNED BOATBUILDER

The excavation and reconstruction of Khufu's barge was an extraordinary venture. Called to head the effort was one of Egypt's leading restorers, Hag Ahmed Youssef Moustafa, who had spent 20 years working on some of the magnificent wall paintings in tombs at Thebes. When he heard of the new find at Giza, he rushed to examine it.

His first glimpse into the pit almost overwhelmed him: "I was anxious and afraid. I knew nothing at all about boatbuilding, and it seemed that this job perhaps needed a shipwright more than it did a restorer."

The initial chores, however, were to open up the pit, remove the ship's more than 1,200 pieces, and, in the process, protect

In the photographs at right, matching hieratic signs—a written version of hieroglyphs—on adjacent timbers confirm that the boards have been properly placed. Four other symbols, also shown in the center drawing, indicate the quarter of the boat to which each piece belongs.

them from deterioration. As each 14-ton limestone slab was lifted away, it was replaced by a block of wood to maintain the temperature and humidity levels within the pit. Boat timbers were then transferred one by one to a restoration shed next to the pit and treated with preservatives. More delicate components such as reed mats and lin-

en rope were soaked in resin to help hold them together.

Meanwhile, Hag Ahmed learned all he could about buil ing wooden ships. Every day f three months he visited boatyards on the Nile to watch loca craftsmen at work; he made sketches, asked questions, and later constructed numerous scale models for practice. By

the time the last pieces had been removed from the pit, Hag Ahmed was ready to tackle the real thing.

He still faced a daunting task. Because the specifics of the ancient boat's design were unknown, it was frequently difficult to tell which pieces went where. Hag Ahmed was guided chiefly by the orderly manner in which the timbers had been buried. Port and starboard planks were often paired, for example, which essentially cut the guesswork in half.

Hag Ahmed and his crew completed five separate reconstructions, each focusing on a particular part of the boat or correcting earlier mistakes. Toward the end of the fourth reconstruction, an assistant realized that symbols on many of the timbers *(left)* actually indicated where they fitted together. Remarkably, only a few corrections had to be made in the final reassembly.

Chief restorer Hag Ahmed Youssef Moustafa works on a small replica of the hull of Khufu's boat. Although he originally intended to use such models to puzzle out the whole ship's construction, he began piecing together actual timbers shortly after the excavation was completed.

A hand-tinted composite image shows the dismantled boat as it appeared when the entire pit was first uncovered in 1955. The timbers were stacked in 13 layers, each of which was carefully photographed and cataloged before being removed.

EXPERT CRAFTSMANSHIP
FOR A SACRED DESIGN

In its final reconstructed form, Khufu's ancient boat testifies not only to the restorers' skill but also to the expertise and artistry of its original builders. Archaeologists, however, agree on little beyond the excellence of its workmanship and its aesthetic charm: The boat's function remains a subject of intense debate.

Experts base their theories on different clues. The vessel's narrow girth and its tapered bow and stern identify it as a papyriform boat, a design mimicking papyrus rafts, whose bunches of reeds were tightly bound together at either end and arched upward. Detail work also reflects the theme: The tops of the thin columns rising from the deck are carved

in the shape of papyrus buds *(far right)*. Probably the earliest type of Egyptian boat, papyrus rafts were traditionally associated with the gods. Some theorists thus speculate that this vessel was intended for Khufu's use in the afterlife, to carry him across the sky in the company of the sun god, Re. Indeed, the ancient Egyptians believed that the sun traveled in such a solar boat during the day, switching to a night boat for its trip through the underworld.

Another school of thought holds that the craft actually once plied the Nile. Some of the hull timbers show signs of having been abraded by the linen ropes used to tie them together—perhaps a result of the wood swelling and the cordage shrinking

when exposed to water. On the basis of this evidence, Hag Ahmed, among others, believes that the boat was part of Khufu's funeral cortege and may have borne his body from Memphis to the royal tomb at Giza. Some contend that it also carried him on sacred pilgrimages and thereby earned the right to be buried as a holy relic. It may even have served in all three capacities.

Whatever its purpose, the craft's elegant lines and the precision of its fittings exemplify the high standards of the Fourth Dynasty, the era of some of ancient Egypt's finest artistic and technical achievements. The boat now resides in a museum built atop the pit in which it lay for so long.

Measuring nearly 150 feet from stem to stern, Khufu's reassembled barge includes a cabin near the stern (far right). A linen canopy may originally have covered both this and the extended open structure.

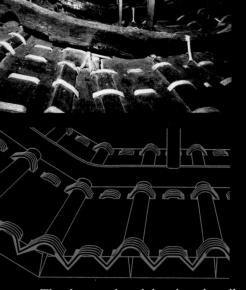

The photograph and drawing above il-
lustrate the over-and-under stitching
that holds the hull together without
piercing the outside. Narrow timbers
lashed directly over the seams between
planks would have sealed the ship
and eliminated the need for caulking.

A museum attendant dusts one of
the five pairs of oars that were found
with the craft. Lacking direct evidence, the restorers could only guess at
the oars' positions and the manner
in which they were lashed.

dreamed that the Sphinx, speaking as Horemakhet (a god combining aspects of Horus and Re), informed him that he would be made king one day if he freed the statue from the sand. Thutmose not only dug out the Sphinx, he also gave it a face-lift: He encased its body with limestone blocks and painted it red, blue, and yellow. As his dream had prophesied, Thutmose became pharaoh. To show his gratitude, Thutmose inscribed a tall granite stele with the story of his dream and placed it between the Sphinx's giant paws.

Later pharaohs built a chapel around Thutmose's stele and repaired the Sphinx's badly eroded legs. By the fourth century AD, however, sand had again engulfed the Sphinx up to its neck. It remained that way until 1818, when Giovanni Caviglia, a Genoese sea captain searching for a rumored hidden entrance, cleared the sand from around the statue's chest. Although he found no opening, he did rediscover the chapel and Thutmose's stele. Twenty years later, the English civil engineer and surveyor John Shae Perring, also searching for a way into the Sphinx, drilled holes into its body. He, too, failed to find an entrance, but the holes, which were not repaired until the 1920s, let rainwater seep into the statue, probably contributing to its deterioration. Both Caviglia and Perring may have been on to something, however, for a Japanese team of investigators, using nondestructive radar and electromagnetic equipment, found tantalizing evidence in 1987 of yet-to-be-explored cavities and tunnels deep beneath the Sphinx.

Three centuries or so after the completion of the Sphinx and the three pyramids at Giza, the great age of pyramid building came to an end in Egypt. Pepi II, whose reign ended centralized power in Egypt for several centuries, erected the final Old Kingdom pyramid at Saqqara. To recapture the glory of the past, pharaohs revived pyramid building during the 12th Dynasty of the Middle Kingdom (2040-1640 BC), but these later kings did not aim to match the more spectacular pyramids of the Old Kingdom. Made primarily of sun-dried mud bricks rather than of stone blocks, the 12th-Dynasty pyramids eventually crumbled into huge mounds of rubble, worn down by years of sun, wind, and Egypt's rare, but heavy, rains.

By the beginning of the New Kingdom, around 1550 BC, pharaohs preferred to be buried in rock tombs in the cliffs near Thebes, the new capital city 325 miles south of Memphis. Egypt's nobility did not completely abandon the old Memphite necropolises,

GIVING THE TIMEWORN SPHINX
A COMPUTERIZED FACE-LIFT

A 15th-century Muslim zealot hacked off its nose; Napoleon's soldiers peppered its head with rifleshot; and in 1988, two chunks of its right shoulder tumbled to the ground. Recently, however, the Sphinx, the majestic lion with the face of a pharaoh, has flashed its enigmatic smile on the computer screen *(right),* expunged of these historical insults.

This electronic restoration began as the brainchild of the American Egyptologist Mark Lehner. Together with his German associate, Ulrich Kapp, he spent many months drawing and measuring the Sphinx from every angle and using a stereoscopic camera lent by Cairo's German Archaeological Institute to take detailed views of the weatherworn, pollution-damaged monument. Then Lehner enlisted the aid of an American architect, Thomas Jaggers, a specialist in computer-aided design, who took the drawings and traced them on a computer screen, entering all the Sphinx's vertical and two-dimensional con-

tours. Over these Jaggers laid more than two and a half million surface points on which to create a "skin." The result was an accurate three-dimensional model that could be manipulated for viewing from any angle.

The next step was to come up with a picture of how the

crouching giant must have looked to the ancient Egyptians. Lehner collected images of several pharaohs, including Khafre, who had had the Sphinx carved from a limestone outcropping 4,500 years ago. Lehner superimposed their features one at a time on the model. "With the face of Khafre," he said, "the Sphinx came alive."

To complete the reconstruction, Lehner studied six steles, or inscribed slabs, dug up at the Sphinx in the 1930s that showed a tall statue of the pharaoh Amenhotep II between the monument's outstretched legs. Today only its pedestal remains. But again, through the magic of the computer, Lehner could put an imaginary version of the work back in place. The statue was apparently erected out of filial devotion by the son of Amenhotep, Thutmose IV, who, more than a thousand years after the Sphinx was carved, initiated its first restoration—and updated it as well by having it painted red, blue, and yellow.

however. At the end of the 18th Dynasty, during yet another revival of interest in the past, royal courtiers and high-ranking administrative and military personnel seem almost to have vied with one another to see who could build the most impressive tombs and funerary chapels at Saqqara. Soon, long streets of these chapels spread across the Saqqara sands, often overlying tombs of the Old Kingdom.

During the later years of the New Kingdom, the Saqqara necropolis also became the site of a most unusual tomb: the Serapeum, a huge multichambered catacomb where the people of Memphis entombed their sacred Apis bulls. The Egyptians saw these animals as the incarnation of the creator god Ptah (later Serapis), and identified them by their special markings. According to the Greek historian Herodotus, who visited Egypt in the fifth century BC, when the cult of the Apis bulls still flourished, the Egyptians believed that a flash of lightning descended from heaven upon a favored cow, "and this causes her to receive Apis." The resulting male calf, he wrote, "has distinctive marks: It is black, with a white diamond on its forehead, the image of an eagle on its back, the hairs on its tail double, and a scarab under its tongue."

Priests fed and tended each Apis bull during its lifetime, giving it the finest foods and stabling and a herd of the best cows. When the bull died, the priests mummified it on a huge alabaster slab in a special temple at Memphis. Then, with great ceremony, funeral attendants transported the bull to the Serapeum at Saqqara, where priests conducted further rituals during the animal's entombment. Once the bull's *ka,* or spirit, had been freed by these rites, a search for the animal's successor began. Much of the elaborate ritual associated with the Apis burials can be traced to Prince Kaemwaset who, in addition to renovating Old Kingdom tombs, served as the high priest of the god Ptah at Memphis and custodian of the Apis.

The cult of the Apis bull probably died out in the second century AD, and the Serapeum gradually disappeared under Saqqara's sands. It was rediscovered in 1851 by the French Egyptologist Auguste Mariette. One day, while walking across the Saqqara plateau, Mariette happened to notice the head of a small sphinx rising from the sand. He suddenly remembered a reference by the ancient Greek geographer Strabo to an avenue of sphinxes at Saqqara. Strabo, who had visited the necropolis in 24 BC, had said that the sphinxes led to an old and sacred tomb for the Apis bulls—the Serapeum.

Buried for almost three and a half millennia, a statue of King Menkaure and his queen emerges from the soil on June 19, 1910. The majestic piece is one of the finest treasures uncovered by the American archaeologist George Reisner and his team while excavating around Menkaure's pyramid, smallest of the three main Giza pyramids.

Gambling his reputation—and the small amount of money the Louvre had allotted him for study—Mariette began his search for the Serapeum. The dig brought immediate success. Mariette uncovered one sphinx after another, as well as various tombs and chapels and several hundred magnificent bronze statues of Apis bulls and other Egyptian deities. Finally, in November 1851, Mariette and his workmen reached the Serapeum itself, sealed behind a decorated sandstone door. With great effort, the workmen removed this final obstacle, and Mariette eagerly entered the tomb's network of underground galleries, which runs for more than 800 feet. "There were numerous vaults," Mariette later wrote. "Some were empty, some contained enormous sarcophagi. I counted twenty-four." The size of these giant granite sarcophagi astonished him: Each measured 13 feet long and 7½ feet wide, and weighed at least six tons—a more than ample size for a mummified bull. The bodies of the once-sacred animals had been stripped of their valuables centuries earlier. But months later, in another group of Apis tombs located in the same area as the Serapeum, Mariette found a vault with an undisturbed sarcophagus of a bull. As he approached the coffin, Mariette saw imprinted in the thick dust on the floor the footprints of the priests who had entombed the animal there 3,000 years earlier.

One of Mariette's most intriguing discoveries involved a wooden coffin found intact, deep within the Serapeum. It contained the mummy of a man, not a bull—probably the only human remains ever to have turned up in the Serapeum. A gilded mask covered the man's face, and he wore a gold chain with two jasper amulets. Both bore the same name: Kaemwaset. When he first saw the amulets, Mariette trembled slightly. "Was this the mummy of the prince Kaemwaset himself before our eyes, the one who was so devoted to the Apis bull?" he later asked.

Modern archaeologists still wonder if the mummy with the golden mask is the body of Kaemwaset, perhaps moved to the Serapeum from its original tomb by Apis cult worshipers hundreds of years after his death. For Kaemwaset was not forgotten by the Egyptian people. Indeed, storytellers handed down tales of his wisdom and love of history for more than a thousand years, even after the last pharaoh had been swept from power and Egypt had become a province of the Roman Empire.

At Saqqara, the first of Memphis's great necropolises, archaeologists continue to make new and exciting discoveries despite the fact that, as the British archaeologist Geoffrey Martin has pointed out, "all of it was plundered and raked over in antiquity—pyramids and temples, as well as private tombs." In 1975, Martin began a search there for the tomb of Maya, overseer of the treasury in the government of the boy-king, Tutankhamen, and one of the most influential officials of his time. The tomb had been found once before, in 1843, by the German Egyptologist Karl Richard Lepsius, but desert sands had soon reburied it. Using Lepsius's map as a guide, Martin and his crew of workmen uncovered a large stone column; Lepsius's map turned out to be off, however, and the column bore not Maya's image and name but that of another, even more powerful Tutankhamen official, Horemheb, an army commander who was destined to become pharaoh himself. Martin subsequently wrote, "We were then convinced that, by a miracle, we had found the long-lost tomb of one of the most famous men of Egypt, Horemheb, whose deeds were well known to scholars

EARTHLY EMBODIMENTS OF THE ANCIENT GODS

The vast cities of the dead under Egypt's shifting sands hold not only human remains but also the mummified bodies of millions of animals, all carefully wrapped in linen, with many of the smaller ones placed in protective pottery jars. These creatures—including bulls, cats, birds, monkeys, rodents, and even insects and eggs—were believed by the Egyptians to embody qualities of specific gods, and because of this divine status were respected in life and buried with ritualistic honor after death.

The animals, however, were not considered actual gods, merely their earthly manifestations. In some cases, every member of a species might be imbued with divinity; all cats, for example, represented the fertility goddess Bast; all ibises and baboons, the wise Thoth; and every falcon, the sky god Horus. Many species appear to have been raised in captivity at various cult centers, ritually killed and embalmed, then sold for offerings to the gods.

In the case of the Apis bull cult, one special male served to represent the god Ptah, and later also Osiris. Identified at birth by certain physical markings, the beast led a pampered life (together with his honored

from many surviving monuments and other sources." Horemheb, who had begun his tomb before he became pharaoh and abandoned it after he rose to power and constructed a new tomb for himself in the Valley of the Kings at Thebes, used it as a final resting place for his first and second wives.

Although plundered centuries earlier by robbers, the Saqqara tomb still contained many beautifully carved reliefs depicting scenes from the general's public career. One shows him receiving rewards from his young pharaoh, whom he served as regent; another reveals him deputizing—a ceremonial job usually only done by a king, which indicates the power Horemheb wielded in Tutankhamen's government. Many military scenes also decorate the tomb, including one of an encampment in which a soldier eats an onion while others roll out dough for bread or fill waterskins from nearby streams. In another chamber, Martin came across the bones of Horemheb's second wife, Mutnodjmet, and those of a fetus or newborn baby, suggesting that the woman had given birth to a stillborn child or died in childbirth.

After excavating Horemheb's tomb, Martin went on to uncover the nearby tombs of the identically named Tia and Tia, sister and brother-in-law of Ramses II, and of several other prominent officials and citizens of New Kingdom Memphis. He had not forgotten, however, his original quest for the vanished tomb of Maya. Then, early in 1986, while crawling through a newly excavated underground passage, Martin and a colleague came upon a stairway leading down to an adjacent, unknown tomb. "A moment or two passed while we negotiated the stairway, being careful not to disturb anything on the way down," Martin wrote. "The ancient robbers must have passed this way on leaving the burial chambers, and there was always the chance that they had dropped something in their anxiety to escape into the fresh air above." But, unlike the robbers many centuries earlier, the two archaeologists took their time. "We were not expecting to find anything dramatic," Martin recalled, "and were concerned at that stage with the prosaic business of maneuvering into position the cable from our generator, located on the desert about 25 meters (82 feet) above our heads. A second or two passed; my Dutch colleague and I held the light bulb above our heads and gazed down beyond the stairway. We were totally unprepared for the sight that met our eyes: a room, full of carved reliefs, painted a rich golden yellow!" Martin's colleague stared at the text of the reliefs with a trained eye. "My God, it's Maya," he cried out. For indeed, the

Apis bulls, like this one crafted in bronze in a 26th-Dynasty votive figure, were venerated throughout Egyptian antiquity, and upon death were buried in large stone sarcophagi.

mother) and was buried with all the pomp of a pharaoh.

Worship of bulls, and animals in general, dates back to the predynastic era, when each village had its own god and totem animals. Some gods and their representatives rose to national importance after the unification of Upper and Lower Egypt, while other cults flourished in small pockets—clear through Greco-Roman times.

inscriptions on the painted walls revealed that the tomb of Tutankh-amen's treasurer had finally been found.

Having located its substructure, Martin and his companion knew that above them must lie the sepulcher's superstructure. Now they were faced with a dilemma: They could empty, as Martin said, "the blocked corridor and penetrate through to the burial chambers (where all kinds of exciting finds might await us) or we could seal the area and the shaft we had discovered by chance and postpone the excavation of the substructure to a future season of work." Had this been the 19th century, when archaeologists took a much more free-wheeling approach to their digging than they do today, Martin might have plunged ahead and gone straight for the yellow room, whose color, linked in the Egyptian mind to the rising sun, symbolized resurrection and rebirth. "Most people—the press certainly—were rather astonished when I opted for the latter expedient," he con-fessed. "How could we possibly contain our impatience for twelve months or more? The reasons are straightforward, even prosaic: Archaeologists are not treasure hunters, the work underground would in any case need careful forethought and planning, and it was logistically more sensible to work from the desert surface downward rather than the reverse." Science had triumphed.

When at last, two years later, Martin penetrated to the interior of the tomb, he found in the havoc created by the robbers centuries ago plenty of evidence that its contents must have been sumptuous. Bits of gold leaf stripped by the thieves from the coffins and other funerary items still lay on the floor, and several links of a gold chain were recovered. Masses of glass inlays and various kinds of stone lay scattered about, along with carved ivory fragments from furniture or boxes. Among the few intact objects were 12 pottery jars, whose sealed lids had been broken off by the thieves in their quest for treasure. When Martin looked inside, he knew why they had not taken them away with them. The vessels contained something too ordinary to bother with—flour and bread.

HOUSES OF ETERNITY

The world's oldest massive stone monuments as well as the most awesome, the pyramids have the power to inflame the imagination. People have always been quick to believe astonishing theories about them. A Scottish astronomer, for example, saw encoded in the Great Pyramid's dimensions not only the distance from the earth to the sun, but the dates of the Hebrews' exodus from Egypt and the projected end of the world—1881.

Serious research is more painstaking—as befits enormous structures built with amazing precision. Each of the four sides of the Great Pyramid, which was constructed for King Khufu more than 45 centuries ago, measures about 756 feet. The difference between the longest and the shortest sides is only 7.9 inches. Not bad for a man-made mountain of some 2,300,000 stones averaging about 5,000 pounds each, soaring to a height of 481 feet, and built without modern tools (not even wheels or iron chisels).

The unimaginable commitment of resources that went into the pyramids attests not only to the power and wealth of Egypt's early rulers, but also to the energy of the tens of thousands of peasant laborers Khufu kept at work for 23 years constructing his pyramid.

For all the permanence that was built into the pyramids, it is ironic that they have yielded little to nature but a great deal to man. Early Egyptians were the first vandals, looting the tombs and removing the limestone sheathing for use in other buildings, a defacing that resumed in later times. With the growth of tourism, decay accelerated. Swarms of intrepid climbers damaged the pyramids and endangered their lives. Thanks to Egyptian laws passed in 1983, the four tiny adventurers above scaling Khufu's pyramid were among the last, although tourists are still allowed inside. Camel drivers and hawkers, who may even have pestered the Greek historian Herodotus as he approached the pyramids, must now keep well back from the monuments.

THE FIRST PYRAMID COMPLEX

The oldest pyramid, the Step Pyramid at Saqqara, in the open desert south of Cairo, grew out of the vanities and abilities of two men—King Djoser and his chief architect, Imhotep. Built around 2630 BC, it exhibited a radical new shape, so new that Egyptians used its silhouette as the hieroglyph for "primeval mound," the first piece of earth to emerge from the soup of creation.

Before the pyramid became the standard tomb for Egypt's early rulers, nobles and high-ranking officials were laid to rest in rectangular, flat-topped sepulchers of mud brick, about 12 feet high, today referred to as mastabas. Djoser's stone tomb probably started out having this shape. Then, as construction progressed and a concept evolved, Imhotep began to place one flat-topped stone structure atop another, continuing until he had created six "steps" by which the king could ascend to the heavens after death. Thus was born the first pyramid—and Imhotep was launched on a career that led later generations to elevate him to the status of demigod. He was certainly Egypt's first great architect in stone, having invented the practice of raising entire buildings in precisely hewn limestone.

Imhotep surrounded Djoser's pyramid with a huge complex of funerary courtyards and chapels and enclosed these with a protective wall running a mile or so in length and rising 33 feet. The complex served as a symbolic setting for the *heb-sed*, a jubilee, or rejuvenation ceremony, that the king had celebrated at court during his reign and was believed to carry on in eternity.

The Egyptians' firm belief in an afterlife was the fundamental force that led to the piling up of stone on such a monumental scale. The Step Pyramid rose to a height of 204 feet, later pyramids even higher. And it was not sufficient that a pyramid be immense; it had to be built so solidly that it would stand forever.

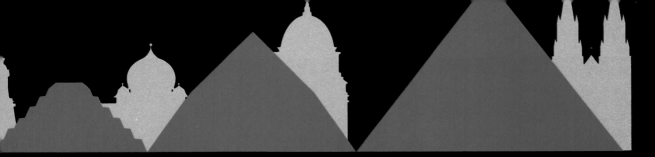

he origin of the world's greatest tombs may have
rung from observations of the earth and its sea-
ns. For as long as human beings had lived in the
lley of the Nile, they had existed under a pact with
ature: In return for the annual enrichment of their
il, they endured the force that gave it to them.
ach year, the mighty Nile brought them the life-
ving essence of Africa in a roiling of brown waters
at inundated their fields for months. But again,
ch year, they looked out across the flood and saw
all mounds poking up—an annual genesis that
played their myth of creation: The earth had
erged, hummock by hummock, from liquid cha-
. Such observations may have led to the reverence
r moundlike structures that led to a national ob-
ssion with pyramids. The Step Pyramid seems to
ve been born of such fundamental belief.

But if a mound represented creation, then the
n was a beacon calling kings to eternal life in a
gher world. On certain days, indeed, when
gged clouds hang over the Eastern Desert, the
n's slanting rays provide the celestial blueprint for
e more familiar pyramid, with its sharply angled
les. Form soon followed philosophy. The Egyp-
ns amended their belief that the spirit of their
ng climbed to the heavens on symbolic steps, and
e royal mode of ascent became sunbeams.

The transition to the sloping sides of the familiar
ramid may have taken place at Meidum, some 40
iles south of the Step Pyramid. Here a tomb of
ven steps was erected. After the addition of an
ghth step, someone had the idea of filling the
aces in between with masonry and encasing the
tire structure in limestone. The result was a tomb
close to a true pyramid as perhaps any that Egypt
d yet seen, but, as it turned out, not one built for

*How do Egypt's pyramids stack up against some of the
world's best-known monuments? In sheer mass, the pyramids
are in a class of their own. The silhouettes above, from left
to right, tell the story in heights:*

- *Statue of Liberty, 303.6 feet*
- *Step Pyramid, 204 feet*
- *Taj Mahal, 313.5 feet*
- *Bent Pyramid, 346.5 feet*
- *Saint Peter's Basilica, 458.7 feet*
- *Great Pyramid of Giza, 481.8 feet*
- *Cologne Cathedral, 518.1 feet*

the ages—in time, the facing stones were stripped
away by looters. King Snefru's Bent Pyramid seems
to reflect another effort to create a true pyramid; it
rises from the desert with sides that are straight
except for one feature: Steep at the base, they
"bend" to a gentler pitch about halfway up.

Thanks to experiments like these, the pyramid
evolved rapidly to its climax in Khufu's giant tomb,
the Great Pyramid, preserving a feature common to
most—a northward-facing entrance. This was done
to align the doorway with the circumpolar stars,
which, seeming never to move in the sky, were
regarded as eternal and thus a suitable terminus for
the king's heavenward journey.

At the time his tomb was built, Khufu, Snefru's
son and successor, inherited a recent theological
development that identified the king with an evolv-
ing cult of the sun. It had a profound influence on
every pyramid that was to come. The king would
accompany Re, the sun god, into the sky. As a cult
text phrased it for him, "May heaven strengthen the
sun's rays for you, so that you may ascend to heaven
as the eye of Re." Thus Khufu's pyramid, the greatest, one of the Seven Wonders of the World,
6,000,000 tons of hand-cut stone covering more
than 13 acres, rose skyward on faith in sunbeams.

The Step Pyramid (top inset) started the fairly rapid evolution of royal burial places from modest tombs to true pyramids. The unique Bent Pyramid (bottom inset) marked the transition to the Great Pyramid (below), the never-to-be-equaled standard that has awed the world.

Little wonder that of the Seven Wonders of the World only the Great Pyramid survives. The others were mere gardens, statues, temples. But stone mountains are expected to outlast everything but geology—even when they are created by mortals.

Sometime after a scholar or tourist catches his or her breath from the first sight of the Great Pyramid come the questions: What is inside? What was its purpose? How was it put there?

In purely physical terms, leaving out the theology, the Great Pyramid was built as an unassailable repository for the mummy of King Khufu. Yet, no matter how his architects strove to seal his burial chamber for all eternity, tomb robbers managed not only to get in but to get away—taking the treasures of the kingdom. They foiled the elaborate, monolithic safeguards of false passages and portcullises set in place to block entry, and overcame whatever superstitions they may have carried into the gloom.

To see or climb a pyramid is one thing. To brave its dark depths is quite another. It isn't simply a matter of following a tunnel to the king's burial chamber. Extra passageways and chambers—some built to store the royal possessions, others meant to confuse robbers—lead off in mystifying directions.

One example of the amazing architectural skill of the pyramid builders is found in the complicated structure above the Great Pyramid's King's Chamber. Five separate compartments are stacked above it, four with flat stone roofs, the top compartment with a pointed roof—all ingeniously designed to distribute the enormous weight of the stones above the burial chamber and keep the sarcophagus from being crushed.

Archaeology has progressed to the point that plans of the interior of the Great Pyramid can be reproduced in detail. Suspicions linger: Is there more? No archaeologist will deny that there might be. The intricate details of the illustration seen here draw on the efforts and finds of generations of archaeologists, including those of Egyptian Zahi Havass, who has located the positions of the Valley Temple and the causeway leading to it, up which the body of Khufu was borne.

The vaulted gorge known as the Grand Gallery (left) ascends eerily to the innermost sanctum of the Great Pyramid of Khufu. Huge stone blocks close in on intruders as the 153-foot passage climbs at a 26-degree angle, ever closer to the burial chamber. The drawing of the Great Pyramid and its funerary complex (right) reveals the architectural secrets within the stone.

Khufu's Eternal Home

1 The Great Pyramid
2 King's Chamber (contains sarcophagus, with stress-relieving spaces in stonework overhead)
3 Queen's Chamber (misnomer)
4 Unfinished chamber
5 Descending passageway (abandoned when burial site was shifted to core)
6 Ascending passageway
7 Grand Gallery
8 "Air" shafts (possibly to link king's spirit to the stars)
9 Mortuary Temple
10 Causeway
11 Valley Temple
12 Eastern boat pits (found empty)
13 Mastabas
14 Enclosure wall
15 Satellite pyramids

THE PHARAOH WHOM HISTORY COULD NOT FORGET

The eerie yet commanding face of the heretical pharaoh Akhenaten forms the upper part of a colossal sandstone statue unearthed at the site of the king's temple to the sun god at Karnak. The exaggerated facial features reflect the revolutionary art style favored by the pharaoh.

One of the best-kept secrets of the ancient world came to light in 1926 at the great religious complex of Karnak at Luxor, part of the long-vanished city of Thebes. For thousands of years, explorers and tourists had poked among the ruins, vibrant with ghostly glories of the remote past. But unknown to them, something was missing—intentionally so. A temple built by the pharaoh Amenhotep IV during the early years of his reign (1353-1335 BC) had been dismantled, piece by piece, and concealed within the walls and foundations of later structures. The eradication of the temple was part of a campaign to eliminate every trace of the hated king—to reject all that he stood for, denying his very existence. In a society obsessed with immortality, his was the worst of all fates: In effect, he had never lived.

The evidence for this extraordinary historical erasure surfaced during a 25-year-long restoration program by the French-sponsored Egyptian Antiquities Service, performed under the direction of the archaeologist Henri Chevrier. While exploring one of the twin massive gateways known as pylons at the Temple of Amen, as well as the substructure of the enormous columned hall, Chevrier recovered more than 20,000 small stone slabs. The blocks were cut to a uniform size, approximately 20 by 10 by 9 inches. Some retained traces of paint; many more were decorated with reliefs that appeared to be fragments of much larger scenes. Because the sandstone blocks were roughly three handspans long, the Egyptian workers took to calling them *talatat,* from the Arabic word for "three." Talatat had been unearthed by earlier excavators, at Thebes and elsewhere, but no one had yet advanced any satisfactory explanation of their origins or meaning.

At the other end of the Karnak complex, Chevrier found more broken masonry incised with Amenhotep IV's name. He concluded that these fragments, along with the talatat found earlier, must have formed part of a demolished temple. Yet the positions of the blocks suggested that they had not been simply knocked down and abandoned, but had been carefully transferred to their present location. Many of the stones showed unmistakable marks of wrath toward the royal family. Portraits of Amenhotep's queen consort, Nefertiti, had been systematically mutilated; some of them, piled one on top of another, had obviously been positioned so that the queen hung upside down. Outside the complex, Chevrier's excavators uncovered the bases of 28 huge statues of Amenhotep IV, along with the shattered remains of 25 of the colossi they had supported, evidence that the figures had been toppled from their pedestals.

T he object of these insults was an 18th-Dynasty pharaoh, scion of a proud line of warrior-kings. In 1550 BC, the founder of his dynasty, Ahmose, had freed Egypt from a century of domination by a tribe of Asiatic invaders. Launching the 500-year era now known as the New Kingdom, Amenhotep's forefathers had forged an empire of unparalleled prestige and power: Their writ ran southward into Africa as far as the Sudan and extended eastward across the Sinai into western Asia. Loyal to their origins, the New Kingdom monarchs had made their ancestral home, Thebes, Egypt's religious capital. On the banks of the Nile, they built great temples, and—three miles away, in a desolate valley at the desert's edge—established their own royal tombs, covering the walls with sculpted reliefs and painted images of themselves and their favored deities.

But Amenhotep IV had departed from the ways of his ancestors. He had abandoned the worship of Egypt's large and complicated pantheon in favor of devotion to a lone Creator, Re, the sun god, manifested by the Aten, a disk that emanated the life-giving rays of the sun. In the fifth year of his reign, the apostate pharaoh an-

Hiding unknown riches, the crumbling ninth pylon of the Amen Temple at Karnak (right) is one of several such gateways that contained thousands of talatat, small stone blocks that once constituted part of Akhenaten's sun-god temple. These had been used as fill after the building was destroyed in a campaign to eradicate the pharaoh's name and memory. The wall painting at top right, from the tomb of an official in the court of Ramses II, shows what a pylon looked like 3,000 years ago, with pennants flying on poles and two white plastered wings flanking a linteled gateway.

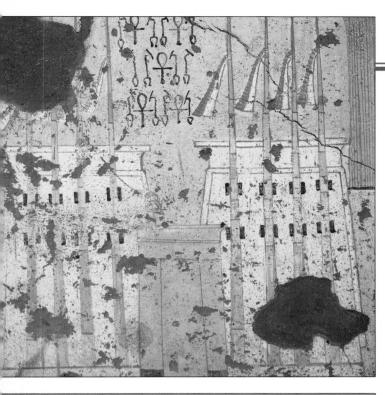

nounced that he would henceforth be known as Akhenaten. The precise meaning of the name is a matter of dispute, but it clearly expresses the king's dedication to his new deity.

Despite the best efforts of Akhenaten, his adoration of the Aten did not take hold in the hearts of the Egyptians. Soon after his death the old gods and goddesses reappeared, once more triumphant, in the tombs and temples of his successors. And, presumably as a punishment for his heresy, the priestly scribes omitted Akhenaten's name from their chronological lists of Egypt's kings. When some allusion to his lifetime was unavoidable, chroniclers made enigmatic references to "the reign of that damned one," or the time of "the rebel."

The task of reconstructing the pharaoh's Aten Temple at Thebes—built when the king was still known as Amenhotep IV—was far beyond the resources available to Henri Chevrier. Workmen stored the thousands of talatat in rough huts, or stacked them on wooden pallets, exposed to the elements. The stones were pretty much gathered up at random, with no record of their original positions or their relationship to any adjacent blocks. Over the years, as additional talatat turned up during restoration or excavation projects, they were simply added to the nearest pile. Individual talatat were carried off the site—either removed by scholars, with official permission, or pilfered by enterprising thieves. Some reappeared in museums and private collections around the world; others vanished altogether.

The result was a seemingly insoluble jigsaw puzzle, incomplete and scattered. Of the 100,000 or so pieces known today, about 35,000 bear some form of surface decoration. They offer tantalizing glimpses of a vanished age—a hand plucking a musical instrument, a queen with arms upraised in some act of adoration, part of a chariot, sculpted faces, ranks of priests or soldiers.

In 1965, Ray Winfield Smith—a retired American diplomat with an interest in Egyptology—hit upon the idea of enlisting computers to solve the riddle of these stones. He proposed using pho-

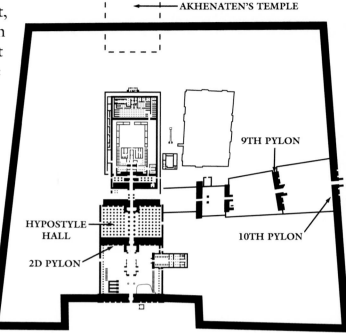

AKHENATEN'S TEMPLE

9TH PYLON

10TH PYLON

HYPOSTYLE
HALL

2D PYLON

tography to make a detailed study of all known talatat, whether they remained on site at Karnak or had been dispersed to foreign collections. He was convinced that researchers could then record and classify every visible attribute of every slab, allowing for all possible permutations and combinations: surviving paint colors; hieroglyphs; human figures with their variations of gender, costume, and gesture; architectural and botanical features; sizes, angles, and positions of lines and shapes; repeating patterns; marks of ancient defacement. The ultimate goal of the project was to find the proper position of every surviving piece of the puzzle and thus reconstruct a model of Akhenaten's original edifice in all its magnificence.

With the blessing of the Egyptian authorities, Smith gathered funds and technical support from institutions around the world and launched the Akhenaten Temple Project. In the team's Cairo office, an Egyptian researcher, Mrs. Asmahan Shoucri, gave a triumphant shout when she made the first successful match—photoprints of two Aten Temple blocks that fitted together to form an image of the rays of the Aten, the sun disk, with a hieroglyphic inscription declaring, "The God's heart is pleased."

With this auspicious blessing from the past, the long and painstaking process of recovery began. Thousands of matches have been made to date, and the detective work still continues, helped by specialists drawn from many different disciplines. Under the auspices of the Akhenaten Temple Project, now headed by the Canadian Egyptologist Donald Redford, new excavations within the Karnak complex have unearthed signs of eight different structures built by the heretic pharaoh to celebrate his monotheistic rites, as well as proof of the steps taken in ancient times to hide them from the light.

Now, despite the best efforts of his enemies, Akhenaten has been rescued from oblivion. Today, few pharaohs seem as intimately known to us, and none is more controversial. More than 3,000 years after he shook Egypt to the core, he still stirs powerful emotions. Within the community of archaeologists and historians, he has as many enemies as defenders. No late-18th-Dynasty priest or palace courtier could have argued more heatedly than do modern Egyptologists over Akhenaten. Was he a madman or a visionary? A saint or a tyrant? Was he a worthy custodian of his forefathers' empire, or the indifferent agent of its decline? One scholar extols him as an enlightened leader; another dismisses him as the prototype of all tin-pot dictators. And every fresh discovery or new interpretation of earlier finds serves only to intensify the debate.

Akhenaten was the son of King Amenhotep III and his chief consort, Queen Tiy. At the time of his birth, the New Kingdom was at its apogee, with a sphere of influence extending far beyond its boundaries. To the south, Nubia lay under the direct control of an Egyptian viceroy, while across the Sinai, in western Asia, tribal chieftains took care to heed the pharaoh's wishes and curry his favor. They regularly

Working inside the ninth pylon, Egyptian laborers remove talatat for stacking elsewhere. The jumbled painted stones below suggest the problem of relating the mismatched blocks to produce coherent visual reconstructions of the decorated walls of Akhenaten's temple.

dispatched caravans laden with tribute, and they sent their sons to be reared at his court, where the foreign princelings learned to identify Egyptian interests as their own.

Farther afield were regional powers who saw themselves as Egypt's equals: the Mitannians in northern Syria, the Babylonians and Assyrians beyond the Euphrates, the Alashians on the island of Cyprus, the Hittites of Anatolia. From the time of Akhenaten's grandfather, Thutmose IV, the rulers of these kingdoms had corresponded with the pharaoh on cordial terms. In their frequent letters they addressed him as "Brother," asked after his health, and offered discreet political advice. They supplemented these missives with pleasing presents—precious objects crafted in silver or lapis lazuli, chariots, musicians and dancers, royal daughters to grace the royal harem. This flow of diplomatic brides was strictly one-way traffic: When the king of Babylon had the temerity to ask Akhenaten's father for an Egyptian princess in return, he was curtly informed that "from of old, a daughter of the king of Egypt has not been given to anyone."

Even the greatest of these foreign potentates could sometimes find himself in financial difficulties. In such circumstances, it was only natural for a hard-pressed king to turn to his beloved friend in Egypt, who enjoyed a virtual monopoly over the known world's supply of gold. "Send gold, quickly, in very great quantities," entreated one lordly neighbor whose sister had been given in marriage to the pharaoh, "so that I may finish a work I am undertaking; for gold is as dust in the land of my brother."

To ensure that envy did not tempt neighbors to acts of folly, Egypt kept its weapons honed and its army ready. But during the reign of Amenhotep III, Egypt was so powerful that no alien state dared risk a war. Without the great military victories that brought glory to his forefathers, the pharaoh had to find other ways to perpetuate his dynasty's muscular, masculine traditions. A minor police action against Nubian raiders, for instance, was extolled—and suitably commemorated in stone—as a resounding personal victory for Amenhotep. Scarabs, engraved by royal command in the early years of the reign, enumerated the young ruler's successes on the hunting field: "Tally of the lions that His Majesty bagged with his own arrows from year 1 to year 10: 102."

Amenhotep III's Great Royal Wife, the mother of Akhenaten, was an impressive person in her own right. She appears even in the marriage contracts recording her husband's diplomatic matches with

Dramatic testimony to the assistance provided by computers in solving the jigsaw puzzle of the talatat, this montage of a portion of wall in Akhenaten's temple was assembled from matches made between keyed photographs of miscellaneous stones. The scene, a depiction of temple life, shows workers carrying jars, milling grain, and feeding cattle.

foreign princesses. The daughter of Yuya, a court official whose clan apparently exercised considerable power, Queen Tiy was the king's first and senior wife: The male children she bore him were the only royal offspring in the line of succession. A doting Amenhotep showered her with gifts, including a man-made pleasure lake at Thebes, vast rural estates, and a temple in Nubia dedicated to her worship.

As were his forefathers, the third Amenhotep was an energetic builder of temples, particularly to Amen—the chief god of Thebes, Egypt's religious capital. As worship of Amen grew, the deity took on aspects of all the many gods in the Egyptian pantheon, particularly Re, the sun god, and became known as Amen-Re. At Thebes, Amenhotep constructed the great Temple of Amen, and added to the god's temple complex at Karnak. To celebrate the jubilee festivals marking three important anniversaries of his reign, he erected an Amen temple and other ceremonial halls at Malkata, in western Thebes.

For the jubilee honoring his 30th year of rule, the pharaoh ordered priests to research the temple archives for the purpose of reconstructing rituals that may have been practiced by the Third- and Fourth-Dynasty kings, more than a thousand years earlier. The fruit of their labors was a ceremony, carefully stage-managed by priests and court officials, in which Amenhotep III was deified in the flesh, transformed into the living incarnation of the ancient sun god, Re. The courtier Kheruef placed an account of the event in his own tomb: "It was His Majesty who did this in accordance with the writings of old. . . . Past generations of people since the time of the ancestors had never celebrated such jubilee rites."

To some scholars, this antiquarian revival represents an attempt by Amenhotep III to inject new life into the state religion. Every reigning pharaoh was seen as a manifestation of the falcon-headed deity Horus, but Amenhotep III may have had higher ambitions, wishing to be worshiped as a god in his own right. But whatever his claims to personal divinity, he could not reign forever. The day came when the priests intoned the ancient formula that announced a pharaoh's death: "The Hawk has flown to Heaven, and another stands in his place." The invocation was intended to reassure, to affirm continuity. But the new hawk apparently had other plans.

The exact date of Amenhotep IV's accession is in dispute, but probably occurred around 1353 BC. Some

HATSHEPSUT: HER MAJESTY THE KING

Long excluded from the top rung of power, women have pressed hungrily into history's leadership vacancies when circumstances have been ripe. Few have been as successful as the great ruler Hatshepsut, whose reign brought Egypt 22 years of peace and prosperity and some of its finest monuments.

A child of Thutmose I, Hatshepsut was about 30 years old in 1479 BC when her husband, Thutmose II, died. The spirited mother of two daughters became regent for her 12-year-old stepson Thutmosee III. In this role she noted that, but for her sex, she would be the rightful heir. Having already overstayed her regency, in 1473 BC she proclaimed herself pharaoh, backed by Senmut, chief steward of the god Amen, a commoner whom she had elevated to high office.

Not wishing to assassinate her

young ward, she recognized him as coregent, allotting him secondary billing on monuments. From then on, she had herself depicted as a man, garbed and bearded like a king, and dubbed His Majesty.

Since kings were regarded as demigods, Hatshepsut enhanced her status by attributing her birth to a union between her mother and the deity Amen and had the lineage inscribed upon a wall of her funerary temple at Deir el Bahri *(below, left)*.

Some time after her death, her stone portraits were shattered and her name erased; who did it and why remains a mystery.

In her own words, Hatshepsut was "beautiful and blooming," an estimate her reconstructed statues do not belie. Her image in red granite *(below)* is one of the few showing her as a woman.

historians believe that the new pharaoh may have ruled jointly with his father for several years; it is known that the reigns of at least four earlier kings overlapped. That the third and fourth Amenhotep may have, for a time, presided over Egypt as coregents has been one of the most intensely argued controversies about the period.

Whether or not his royal father still lived, the new king did not launch his religious revolution overnight. Yet it soon became clear that, apart from the sun god, the deities of Egypt, in all their hundreds of names, aspects, and shifting shapes, did not interest him. Increasingly, he focused his own personal devotion—and soon his very name—on the solar deity he called the Aten, the life-giving sun.

In a Great Hymn to the Aten, the king extolled the sun disk and declared that he was its only earthly intermediary: "Living Aten, Beginner of Life. . . . Thou art in the sight of men, yet thy ways are not known. . . . How manifold are thy works! They are hidden from the sight of men, O Sole God, like unto whom there is no other! Thou didst fashion the earth according to thy desire. . . . Thou art in my heart, but there is none other who knows thee save thy son Akhenaten. Thou hast made him wise in thy plans and thy power."

These and other texts, commissioned or composed by Akhenaten, made it clear that the obligation of ordinary mortals was to worship the pharaoh as the conduit of Aten's power. The new faith apparently did not concern itself with rules for human conduct. Nevertheless, in the view of some scholars, his hymns and invocations reveal Akhenaten as a pioneer of monotheism, a precursor of Abraham and Moses. Others argue that Akhenaten was not a reformer but an ultraconservative, perpetuating Amenhotep III's devotion to the sun god in a more extreme form, and continuing the efforts of his father to regain the fully divine status Egypt's kings had enjoyed in earlier times. Whatever his motives, Akhenaten intensified his campaign to transform the state religion. On the walls of one of his new temples at Thebes, he not only sang the praises of the Aten, but also enumerated the failings of the old deities he wished to discredit. Perhaps as early as the fifth year of his reign, he rocked the religious establishment by banning the worship of the entire Egyptian pantheon—especially Amen—and ordering the closure of temples throughout his dominions.

The priests of Egypt were horrified. Under the old regime,

This statue—believed by some scholars to represent Akhenaten, by others his wife Nefertiti—may have worn a kilt.

they had enjoyed unparalleled prestige and power. Throughout the 18th Dynasty, their temples to Amen had dominated the economic life of the realm. Tithes and tributes flowed into Amen's treasuries, and the god's granaries held the nation's surplus grain. The Amen priesthood sent its own trading missions to foreign parts and controlled the labor forces for public works at home.

But a pharaoh could not be openly defied. Presumably, the priests of Amen stood by while their cult images were destroyed by royal command. The more perspicacious of them may have tailored their beliefs in accordance with the pharaoh's own. And when he introduced a new version of the jubilee festival, honoring the Aten, there were certainly priests in attendance at the ceremony.

To worship his god, Akhenaten built shrines at Thebes, next door to the great Amen Temple. In a complex that may have been more than half a mile long, the pharaoh honored the sun disk under the open sky, in broad courts filled with sacrificial altars. The walls of these shrines glowed with massive, brilliantly colored relief carvings of Akhenaten, Nefertiti, and their daughters, seen in direct communication with the Godhead. The sun's rays reached down from above in these images, extending anthropomorphic hands to touch the king with the *ankh*—the symbol of life.

Nefertiti played a prominent role in the celebration of the cult. A tally of the reliefs in the remains of a temple built for her use reveals that her name and image appeared at least twice as often as those of the king. Inscriptions found at Karnak and elsewhere honor her with a list of fulsome epithets: Great of Favor, Mistress of Sweetness, Beloved One, Mistress of Upper and Lower Egypt, Great King's Wife Whom He Loves, Lady of the Two Lands.

Nefertiti's daughters also took part in the worship of the Aten. The eldest girl was probably born shortly before her father ascended the throne. In images dating from the earliest years of the reign, she appears as a toddler, dressed in a miniature version of her

mother's costume and shaking the sistrum—a musical instrument used in religious rites throughout Egypt's history. The caption to the scene announces her as "the king's bodily daughter whom he loves, Meretaten, born of the great king's wife Nefertiti, may she live." Within a few years, Meretaten is joined in the reliefs by two sisters, Meketaten and Ankhesenpaaten. If there were sons born of Nefertiti and Akhenaten's union, they do not appear in any family scenes.

A few students of the reign have cast doubt on Akhenaten's ability to father any child at all. They interpret the odd, often androgynous, features in his portraits—rounded hips and breasts, elongated face, impossibly slender neck, spindly legs, and slack belly—as symptoms of a glandular disorder that would have rendered him sterile. Opponents of this view argue that the king specifically instructed his artists to represent him with these bodily distortions as visible symbols of his divinity. The presence of the same characteristics in reliefs of Nefertiti and the princesses are interpreted by some scholars as a statement that they too were more than merely mortal. However, the images of virtually all of Akhenaten's followers—even servants and military guards—seem to display similar traits.

This strange-looking royal family first came to the notice of the modern world on a stark, sun-bleached site in Middle Egypt 240 miles north of Thebes. Here, at a place now known as Tell el Amarna—or simply el Amarna—the limestone cliffs on the east bank of the

Nile recede to form a natural amphitheater, a basin of rock embracing eight miles of sandy plain. In the early 1820s, European travelers were drawn to this austere location by reports of oddly decorated burial chambers cut into the cliffs. In 1824 and 1826, the Englishman John Gardner Wilkinson— who came to Egypt in hopes that its warm climate would improve his health and stayed to explore the antiquities that had captured his imagination—made copies of some of the reliefs in the tombs. At the time of these visits, the science of deciphering hieroglyphs was in its earliest infancy; but even without being able to read the inscriptions, it was obvious to Wilkinson that he was in the presence of something extraordinary.

Within the tombs, the ancient sculptors had deviated from the artistic conventions of their age. Instead of stylized battlefield ballets and gloomy voyages into the realm of the dead, they had depicted what appeared to be intimate scenes in the daily life of a royal couple—who were only much later identified as Akhenaten and Nefertiti. The subjects enjoyed their domestic ease, lounged in chairs with their infant daughters in their laps, and took part in family feasts.

Many carvings depicted some kind of religious ceremony; yet curiously, the gods of Egypt's pantheon were nowhere to be found. No falcon-headed Horus, horned Hathor, somber Osiris, or any other deity appeared at el Amarna. The only visible object of worship was a more abstract symbol of divine power: a great disk, hanging in the heavens, emanating multiple rays that ended in human hands, apparently directing some form of benediction at the king and queen.

Other Europeans followed Wilkinson, making surveys of the tombs in the northern cliffs and clearing the sand from burial places at the southern end of the site. In 1843, and again in 1845, the great German Egyptologist Karl Richard Lepsius—one of the earliest find-

In a scene of domestic bliss carved on a limestone block, Akhenaten and Nefertiti bask in the rays of the Aten, the sun god, as they play with their daughters. The rays, bearing the breath of life, are aimed symbolically at the royal couple's faces.

An unfinished limestone sculpture shows Akhenaten affectionately holding and kissing one of his daughters. Such representations were intended not only to suggest familial devotion, but also to demonstrate the blessed state in which the royal family lived as direct recipients of the sun god's beneficence.

ers of talatat at Thebes—visited el Amarna with a survey team. In one 12-day marathon of intensive copying, the team garnered enough material to occupy generations of researchers.

It was observed that the cartouches—decorative frames containing the names of the pharaoh and his queen—had been defaced to conceal their identities. But some of these labels remained just barely legible. By the time of Lepsius's visit, the understanding of hieroglyphs had advanced sufficiently to allow scholars to decipher what was left of the inscriptions.

The tombs appeared untenanted; no evidence of burials was found. But they were only part of the mystery that began to unfold at el Amarna. The bleak plain contained a great many dark mounds, beneath which lay ruined palaces, temples, homes, and workshops—the remnants of a lost city called Akhetaten, meaning "horizon of the Aten," founded by Akhenaten as a new royal capital and a religious center for the Aten cult. But there were no signs of continuous settlement on the site. Apparently, Akhenaten had built on virgin territory, and just a few years after his death, his city had been abandoned to the jackals.

Despite the occasional visits of British, German, and French Egyptologists to el Amarna, organized excavations did not begin until late in the 19th century, when interest was kindled by a chance discovery. In 1887, a woman from one of the modern villages in the vicinity of el Amarna was digging for *sebakh*—the nitrogen-rich compost into which ancient mud bricks decay—when she unearthed a cache of more than 300 small clay tablets. Local dealers in antiquities were uncertain what to make of the objects, which were inscribed with mysterious wedge-shaped symbols. Dismissed as fakes, the tablets passed from hand to hand; some were broken, others disappeared. Eventually, a few specimens came to the attention of E. A. Wallis Budge, a representative of the British Museum. "I felt certain," he later said, "that the tablets were both genuine and of very great historical importance."

Budge recognized the inscriptions as cuneiform, and he identified the documents as consisting largely of letters, most of which were written in Akkadian, the tongue of Babylonia and the international diplomatic language of Akhenaten's day.

The fragment of painted floor above from a palace at Akhenaten's capital, Akhetaten, reflects the naturalism that distinguished art during his relatively short reign. The papyrus and lotus plants seem to sway in the breeze, while the papyri portrayed at left in an earlier painting stand stiffly in rows, demonstrating the rigidity of most traditional Egyptian art.

The missives had come from the rulers of various kingdoms in western Asia. The cache was a remnant of Akhetaten's diplomatic archives, left behind when the capital was abandoned. The voices of these alien kings helped break the conspiracy of silence surrounding Akhenaten's reign.

In 1891, the British archaeologist Flinders Petrie began work at the site of Akhetaten, investigating the remains of two temples to the Aten, several private houses, the Great Official Palace of Akhenaten, and the Bureau of Correspondence, where the Amarna tablets had been found. Ancient robbers had made a fairly thorough job of plundering the site, but Petrie's study of the fragments they left behind revealed that Akhenaten's palace had been an edifice of considerable splendor. Its walls, when new, would have glittered with colored glass, stone, and ceramic inlays; its columns were crowned with palm-leaf capitals whose details were picked out in red, blue, and gold; its walls were covered with stone slabs of many colors, inlaid with hieroglyphs formed from obsidian, black granite, red quartzite, limestone, and glass. Glazed tiles displayed painted gardens of plants and flowers and aquariums of swimming fish.

In a section of the palace that Petrie identified as the harem, he came upon a painted plaster floor of great beauty. To preserve it, he mixed up some tapioca water and then applied it with the side of his finger. But since there were 250 square feet to cover, he could work only intermittently—or his skin would have worn away. Despite Petrie's efforts to preserve an architectural feature that had remained intact for more than three millennia, the floor fell victim to an act of vandalism. Some years after Petrie found it, a local villager, fed up with sightseers tramping across his fields to view it, hacked up the plasterwork. Enough pieces survived, though, for them to be taken to the Cairo Museum and given a home there.

Some of Petrie's most valuable discoveries came not from the remains of important buildings but from the ancient refuse dumps he sifted with scrupulous care. He found fragments of jars that had once held oil, meat, or wine; inscriptions upon the pottery shards and seals affixed to them provided information about places of origin and dates of shipments. Wine jars, marked with the year of vintage and the estate from which they had come, enabled Petrie to determine the duration of Akhenaten's reign: The last year noted

The carved image on this limestone fragment from Akhetaten depicts a hand releasing a lump of incense or scented fat, perhaps as an offering. The exquisitely rendered fingers—possibly the pharaoh's own—express the ideal of elegance that marked the art of the period.

was the 17th of the pharaoh's rule. Other dated labels indicated that his successor, Smenkhkare, was king for no more than three years after Akhenaten's death; the absence of any items marked with the names of later monarchs confirmed that Akhetaten was abandoned soon thereafter.

It was clear that Akhenaten had imagined a far more glorious future for his new capital when, five years into his reign, he commanded squads of architects and surveyors to plan this ideal city. In the rock on both sides of the Nile, sculptors carved 14 boundary markers proclaiming the establishment of the capital, each decorated with an image of the royal family.

A contemporary account of the ceremonies inaugurating Akhetaten lists sacrificial offerings of "bread, beer, long- and short-horned cattle, wild game, fowl, wine, fruit, incense, libations, and all fine vegetables," and describes how the nobles, senior army officers, and "the great ones of the palace" came to do homage, at the pharaoh's command. "They were quickly ushered in to him. Then they were on their bellies before him, kissing the earth in his presence. Said His Majesty to them: See Akhetaten, which the Sun Disk wishes to have built for himself as a memorial in his own name." The king then spelled out the plans for the new capital and described some of the principal official buildings: a House and Mansion of the Sun Disk, a House of Rejoicing, royal apartments, and a Sunshade for the queen. The solemnities concluded with a tour of the perimeters of Akhetaten by the pharaoh, riding in his gleaming chariot of state. At each boundary stone, he swore an oath dedicating himself to the site, vowing that upon his death he would be buried at this sacred city.

Before the paint was dry or the stonecutters' dust had settled, Akhenaten moved his household and court to the new location, taking up residence in temporary quarters—probably a collection of spacious tents. In its finished state, Akhetaten offered a theatrical setting for celebrating the rites of divine kingship. Mounting his chariot, and followed by his entourage of courtiers, priests, guards, and outriders, the pharaoh would pass in procession along the road that linked his secluded and well-fortified private residence to the Great Aten Temple and to his Great Palace, a complex of stately halls and courts adorned with colossal statues of his royal personage. In these imposing settings, he worshiped the Aten, received delegations of foreign envoys, and showed himself to his people at the balcony known as the Window of Appearance, tossing down gold ornaments and other gifts to those followers he wished to honor.

In the first few years of the city's existence, the population grew to somewhere between 20,000 and 50,000—noblemen, priests, bureaucrats, traders, artisans, boatmen, and their families. A police force, including both foot patrols and a chariot corps, kept order. The headquarters building—complete with stables—was identified 3,000 years later by the mud bricks stamped with its name. Deep wells were sunk to serve those parts of the city distant from the riverside. Brewhouses and bakeries, run by the temple, produced beer and bread to provide the necessary offerings to the Aten.

Although the courtiers closest to Akhenaten built mansions in the shadow of his palace, the different classes making up the city's population were mostly intermingled. A chief charioteer named Ranefer possessed a modest corner house a short walk away from the more imposing home of Ramose, a senior army officer. Nakht, the pharaoh's vizier, or first minister, chose a site at the very opposite end of the city from the palace, where he constructed a house adorned with handsome columns. Proprietors carved their names and titles upon their doorframes and gateposts; a few of these have survived.

The most affluent families lived in villas set in walled grounds. Trees and flowers grew in gardens adorned with ponds and small shrines. Indoors, there was sufficient space for public reception halls and private living quarters, including bathrooms equipped with drainage holes in the floor. Humbler houses were on a smaller scale

In this masterpiece, carved on a limestone slab, two horses stand before a chariot (not shown). *The horse was a common theme in Egyptian art, but here Akhenaten's artist gave it spirit and freshness through the simple device of having one horse lower his head to bite his itching foreleg.*

but built to a similar design. Most were single-story structures, topped with a flat roof that provided additional sleeping space in warm weather. The kitchen was as far away as possible from the main domestic quarters, preferably downwind. In the yard, circular granaries held supplies of wheat and barley, and a small shed might house a cow or a goat.

Artisans' homes doubled as workshops. In the main city, for instance, the chief sculptor, Thutmose, lived in a complex that held his own house, a studio, and quarters for his staff of workmen. Here he produced portrait studies of the royal family, to be used as models for public monuments and private shrines. When the city was abandoned, the last occupants of the sculptor's house left some of his unfinished works and models behind. In time the building collapsed, and blown sand covered these forgotten pieces.

On a December day in 1912, they were found by a team of German archaeologists, headed by Ludwig Borchardt. One of the trophies was a modeled head of Nefertiti. She was dazzling, with a slender neck, elegant features, and a tranquil gaze. Her charisma, helped by Thutmose's art, leaped across the generations. She would, in time, become the most evocative symbol of her long-ago world. On the night after the discovery, Borchardt sat down to compile the log of objects found that day. But he knew it was impossible to record the details with his usual professional detachment. "I wrote," he later confessed, " 'Description futile: Must be seen.' "

In her magnificence, the sculpted Nefertiti represented an age of creative innovation and experimentation. The stylistic changes that began to evolve at Thebes during the first years of the reign gained momentum with the transfer of the court to Akhetaten. Sculptors explored the play of light and shadow, and combined different materials to achieve new textures. Human subjects sprang to life, rendered much as they looked. The natural world was vividly represented. Plants and animals came to life on painted floors and ceramic tiles, or as jeweled ornaments and glass figurines.

The most vibrant of the surviving sculptural art at el Amarna is found in its decorated tombs, yet there is no sign that any of these ever housed an actual burial. For his own tomb, Akhenaten chose a position removed from the rest, in a cleft of the eastern hills. It would

Stele "S" is one of 14 steles, or boundary markers, that Akhenaten had chiseled into stone cliffs on both sides of the Nile to demarcate his new capital. The carved relief shows the king and queen raising their hands in adoration of the sun disk. The inscription reads in part: "The great and living Aten, vigorously alive, my father, my reminder of eternity."

be found in the late 19th century by the Italian archaeologist Alexandre Barsanti. Within the royal burial place, reliefs on the walls of two or three chambers recorded moments of public celebration and private grief. One room portrayed the death of a young princess—or possibly one of the pharaoh's secondary wives—in childbirth. As the surviving infant is borne away by a nurse, the king, queen, and court wail, raise their arms to heaven, and scatter dust upon their heads.

To reward his courtiers, Akhenaten presented them with tombs in two cemetery complexes on the escarpment to the east of the city. The recipients of this honor included the palace physician, Pentu, the priest Pinhasy, and Ay, Royal Master of the Horse, who would later rise to become pharaoh. On the walls, reliefs showed the tomb owners engaged in acts of reverence, adoring the god-king as the intermediary of the Aten. But the reliefs also provide glimpses of the life of the reign—scenes of award ceremonies, vignettes of royal family life, massed offerings of food and flowers. Inscribed prayers and hymns praised the god-king as the source of all well-being:

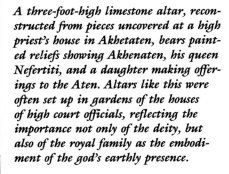

A three-foot-high limestone altar, reconstructed from pieces uncovered at a high priest's house in Akhetaten, bears painted reliefs showing Akhenaten, his queen Nefertiti, and a daughter making offerings to the Aten. Altars like this were often set up in gardens of the houses of high court officials, reflecting the importance not only of the deity, but also of the royal family as the embodiment of the god's earthly presence.

LIVING FACES FROM THE SANDS OF TIME

The sculptor Thutmose had a lot going for him, including royal patrons and the spanking new house shown above, complete with master bedroom, bathroom, workshop studios, and large silos for storing his accumulated wealth in grain. But with the death of Akhenaten and the reversion of the capital from the specially built city of Akhetaten to Thebes, all this changed, and Thutmose's house was abandoned.

Over the years the works the sculptor and his assistants left behind in the studios, some of which are reproduced here, were buried under drifting sands as the mud-brick walls crumbled away, not to come to light again until this century when archaeologists unearthed them. Among the relics was the famous painted limestone bust of Akhenaten's queen Nefertiti, seen below. Apparently Thutmose had deliberately left the portrait unfinished as a demonstration model, with the empty socket used to show students how a glass eye should be inserted. To the right of the bust can be seen another study of the queen—perhaps also a teaching model—that still bears the sculptor's painted guidelines.

The serene images of Nefertiti found at the site—there were several—suggest that Thutmose idealized her features somewhat as he strove after elegance in keeping with the art style that blossomed during Akhenaten's reign. But also

present in the workshop were studies of individuals whose identities are unknown that, by contrast, startle with the force of their realism. Like the two plaster faces at the lower right, these are images of living, breathing Egyptians, free of all artistic convention.

Debate continues among scholars as to Thutmose's intentions here, but the most likely theory is that the masklike pieces were life studies taken from casts made directly on the faces of the subjects, possibly in two parts (seams down the middle of some suggest a joining). Perhaps it was from "photographic" models like these that Thutmose then created his stone sculptures, perfecting the features for the appreciation of a broader audience.

"Grant that I may be satisfied with seeing thee without ceasing; this lord who like Aten forms a full Nile every day, making Egypt live."

While the sculptors plied their hammers and chisels at the necropolis, the court pursued its business in the central city. At the Bureau of Correspondence, scribes translated and filed the communications sent to Akhenaten by foreign kings. The world beyond Egypt's borders was in turmoil. In Syria, the newly powerful Hittites flexed their muscles, winning territory from Egypt's old friends, the Mitannians, and worrying its other West Asian allies. Suppiluliumas, the Hittite ruler, had made friendly gestures to Akhenaten, beginning with a congratulatory letter upon his coronation, but the king of Cyprus warned the pharaoh to be wary of these advances: "Do not bind yourself to the king of the Hittites!"

When the Hittites marched upon them, small kingdoms that had considered themselves under Egypt's protection begged for help. Akizzi, ruler of Qatanum, wrote on behalf of four fellow monarchs, pleading that Akhenaten—if unwilling to come himself with an avenging army—at least send reinforcements, and offered to pay any price: "They say that the king my lord will not march out. So let my lord dispatch archers, and let them come. Let my lord's ministers say what shall be their tribute and they shall pay it." But no help was sent, and Suppiluliumas soon stood on the plains of Aleppo to receive the homage and tribute of these newly conquered kings, who would now become his vassals instead of Akhenaten's. Word came to Akhetaten: "All the servants of the king my lord have gone away to the Hittites."

There may have been sound tactical reasons for Akhenaten's apparent unwillingness to respond—the archives uncovered at el Amarna did not contain the Egyptian side of any correspondence, which would have been sent written on papyrus. In the view of some scholars, however, the king was too preoccupied with his religious obsessions to look to the outside world. Displaying few signs of the military virtues cultivated by his forefathers, he seemed more interested in directing the works of his artists and worshiping his god than in leading his army.

Nevertheless, Egypt's prestige could not have been a matter of indifference to Akhenaten. The Amarna tombs record an elaborate ceremony, held in the 12th year of the reign, when the king received delegations of envoys bearing tribute. The tombs of Huya, high steward of the dowager queen, Tiy, and of Meriri II, overseer of the harem, contain a record of this event. Their reliefs show the royal family, attended by courtiers, servants, fan bearers, and military escorts, receiving gifts from the ambassadors. An inscription records how Akhenaten and Nefertiti arrived at the ceremonies, borne aloft on the great golden state palanquins, or litters, which must have glowed like the disk of the Aten itself, dazzling the eyes of beholders. The exotic treasures carried before the royal couple represented the finest offerings that Egypt's neighbors could provide, sent from "Syria and Kush, the West and the East, all lands united at the one time, and the Isles in the midst of the Great Green Sea."

The event may not have been an unmitigated delight for the foreign dignitaries in attendance. The pharaoh reveled in the warmth of his heavenly parent, but some visitors to his court went home with complaints. King Ashuruballit I of Assyria boldly demanded of Akhenaten: "Why are my messengers kept standing in the open sun? They will die in the open sun. If it does the king good to stand in the open sun, then let the king stand there and die in the open sun. Then will there be profit for the king!"

Some of the pharaoh's loyal subjects may have privately agreed with Ashuruballit. But if they thought an excess of the Aten's rays had addled the royal brains, they did not say. Yet when, in the 17th year of his reign, Akhenaten died—apparently of natural causes—they made little effort to perpetuate his religious reforms.

Controversy surrounds his immediate successor. In recent years, some historians have suggested that Nefertiti assumed the crown for a while before it passed to Smenkhkare, who survived Akhenaten by as much as three years. Other scholars claim Smenkhkare immediately followed Akhenaten. Smenkhkare may have been the king's younger brother, and his route to the throne could have been through marriage to the eldest of Akhenaten's daughters. The question of whether Nefertiti ruled, however briefly and covertly, before Smenkhkare is further confused because it has been argued that the skeletal remains thought to be Smenkhkare are not Smenkhkare at all, but Akhenaten himself. Whatever the case, comparative anatomical evidence indicates that the remains now identified as Smenkhkare are of a blood relation of the next pharaoh in line—the considerably more famous Tutankhamen.

The accession of Tutankhamen—a child of nine at the time—heralded the complete restoration of the old state religion. A proclamation, issued in the name of the new monarch, deplored the condition of the realm, with its temples decayed, its people discouraged, and its gods so angered that they had turned their backs on Egypt. To the satisfaction of the priestly establishment, the old gods were brought back to hold sway once more. And, to confirm the fact that a new broom now swept the realm, Tutankhamen also declared that the city of the sun disk should be abandoned.

Leaving no record of any regrets, the inhabitants of Akhetaten gathered their worldly goods and departed. Nothing they deemed of any use was left behind. The scribes at the Bureau of Correspondence may have decided that their files of foreign letters represented excess baggage: They left them at Akhetaten, there eventually to be buried

General Horemheb, who would become pharaoh and in that capacity do more to obliterate Akhenaten's memory than anyone else, wears coiled gold necklaces bestowed by his then-king, Tutankhamen. On his head is an ornamental cone, common for the day, consisting of a mixture of fat and perfume that gradually melted to scent both his wig and his presence.

by the sands—destined to lie undisturbed in this sun-bleached ghost town until the peasant woman brought them once again to light.

After reigning for less than a decade, Tutankhamen died. The crown passed to Ay, an elderly but ambitious official who married Akhenaten's eldest surviving daughter, Ankhesenamen. Some historians think he may even have been Queen Tiy's brother and Nefertiti's father—which, if true, means that he married his own granddaughter, a not-so-unthinkable liaison in the complicated realities of Egyptian politics and bloodlines. Ay had been an important figure in the court of Akhenaten, as is indicated by an inscription in his tomb: "I was one favored by his lord every day. My name has penetrated into the palace, because of my usefulness to the king, because of my hearing his teaching." But times had changed. Eradication of the memory not only of the heretic pharaoh but also of his immediate successors began. Ay resumed the building projects at Karnak that Akhenaten, as Amenhotep IV, had started, erasing the pharaoh's name and adding his own to them. Even inscriptions honoring Tutankhamen were scraped away and replaced with the cartouches of Ay during the latter's brief reign of some four years.

The real work of writing Akhenaten out of history was undertaken by the next pharaoh. Horemheb was a military man, commander in chief of the army after the death of Akhenaten. Apparently to secure his own place in the royal succession, he married Mutnodjmet, sister of Nefertiti and perhaps also a daughter of Ay. At the Amen temple complex at Karnak, he engraved in stone his intention to purge Egypt of the rot that had set in during the reign of Akhenaten. Every plague upon the realm, from thieving tax collectors to corrupt judges, was to be eradicated. But, most importantly, the name of the pharaoh who had launched this degradation and lost Egypt the love of its old gods was to be wiped from the records. Even the stone walls of the temples the heretic had built to his fraudulent Aten were to be tumbled to the ground.

To carry out this royal command, a foreman at Karnak mustered his demolition gang and raised his staff of office. As he tapped the rod against a wall, or perhaps lifted it to strike a sluggish worker, the small knob at its tip—bearing the cartouche of Horemheb—broke off and fell into the mounting pile of rubble. In AD 1978, the Egyptologist Donald Redford would find it, amid the remnants of Akhenaten's temple to his forgotten god.

THE STORIES MUMMIES TELL

Of the many relics bequeathed to the world by the Egyptians, none are more fascinating than their mummies. Here are the almost lifelike remains of real people—commoners as well as kings—who lived and died long before Europeans could call themselves civilized. The 3,200-year-old body of Ramses II, for example, is so well preserved that even his individually wrapped toes *(above)* survive intact.

Mute witnesses to their times, mummies nevertheless have stories to tell about life in ancient Egypt, stories that scientists studying them extract from their bones and flesh through use of various modern medical techniques including x-rays, CAT scans, and forensic autopsies. Specialists have even been able to reconstitute blood cells and use them to trace kinship. Thus when blood samples of Tutankhamen matched up with those taken from the body of an unidentified male who resembled the boy-king, scientists could posit that the mummy belonged either to Smenkhkare, thought by some to be Tutankhamen's older brother, or to his supposed father, the pharaoh Akhenaten. In the future, it may be possible to take DNA from cells of ancient Egyptians and use the genetic information it contains to confirm family connections.

Mummies show that most Egyptians did not live long, dying between the ages of 35 and 40 from a variety of ailments and diseases. Occasionally they yield poignant evidence of thwarted lives. The skeletal remains of 18th-Dynasty Queen Mutnodjmet turned up with those of a baby, suggesting that she died in childbirth at age 42, a dozen years after marrying Pharaoh Horemheb, a commoner who had taken the throne. The physical anthropologist studying her bones found extensive trauma to her pelvis, indicative of multiple births. But since records reveal Horemheb had no heir, her babies must have been born dead or died shortly after delivery. The scientist theorized that during her marriage Mutnodjmet may have been pregnant 13 times, and that as a result of her frustrated efforts to bear a prince before menopause, she grew progressively anemic, until her last pregnancy claimed her life.

Had Mutnodjmet given birth to a living son, history might have been different. If, as some think, she was the sister of Queen Nefertiti, her offspring would have added a legitimacy to Horemheb's reign, and the 18th Dynasty, one of Egypt's most glorious, would have continued. Instead, it came to an abrupt end with Horemheb's death around 1310 BC.

THE ETERNAL ONES

Thanks to two incredible finds made in the late 19th century, most of the bodies of the pharaohs of the 18th, 19th, and 20th dynasties survive to this day. Their mummies, along with those of many of their queens, were discovered in two secret caches, where they had been hidden almost 3,000 years ago by priests eager to protect them from tomb robbers.

As well preserved as the 90-year-old Ramses II *(right)* were his father, Seti I *(below)*, and Yuya and Tuya *(opposite)*, parents of Queen Tiy, wife of Amenhotep III. X-rays of his head showed that Ramses was, as one specialist put it, "a dental cripple." Not only did he have heavily worn back teeth, but he also had tooth abscesses and severe periodontitis. In addition, he had heart disease, hardening of the arteries, and arthritis of the hips and spine that gave him a bent posture. Analysis of his long, wavy hair revealed a surprising fact: In younger years the almost six-foot-tall pharaoh had had an auburn mane.

On display in Paris, where it had been sent for conservation in 1975, the mummy of Ramses II (above) lies before a backdrop of a wall relief depicting him as a chariot-driving warrior in the vigor of his youth. The mummy of his father, Seti I (left), wears a collar fashioned by priests after robbers knocked off the head in a search for valuables hidden in the wrappings.

Found in their own tomb, Yuya, Master of the King's Chariots, and his wife Tuya, are among the best preserved of all mummies. Yuya's features suggest he may have been of eastern Mediterranean origin. Originally courtiers, the couple acquired higher status when their daughter Tiy married a king.

MEDICAL DIAGNOSES FOR THE LONG DEAD

Mummies have much to say about the interplay between the Egyptians and their environment. Their lungs show blackening from the smoke of lamps and heating and cooking fires, a condition that left many with anthracosis, a disability of coal miners today. More prevalent was silicosis, a disease caused by breathing dust during desert storms.

Wind-blown sand, as well as particles from grinding stones, got into grain and flour, producing gritty bread that wore teeth down. Rapid tooth wear led to invasion of root canals by bacteria. Gum and jaw abscesses, in turn, lowered resistance—and, upon spreading to the neck, could bring death.

The very Nile, the giver of life during its annual flooding, could also take life, as is demonstrated by the remains of various river-borne parasites often found in mummies. These were introduced into victims through food and drinking water or by direct exposure to microscopic larvae. One virulent parasite, the bilharzia worm, which attaches itself to blood vessels, could be picked up by adults and children wading in canals and along the muddy banks of the Nile. Among those it invaded, it caused slow mental and physical decline.

The deformed foot of the 19th-Dynasty pharaoh Siptah was long thought to be congenital. But an x-ray revealed bone deformities and atrophied muscles indicative of polio, which the king must have contracted in his youth. The foot stretched to compensate for the shortened leg.

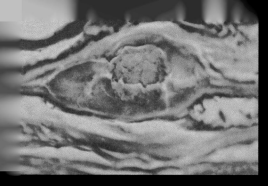

Three samples of medical evidence obtained from mummies include a Trichinella cyst (top left), produced by the parasite found in undercooked, infected pork; rehydrated type-B red blood cells (left); and grit-worn teeth.

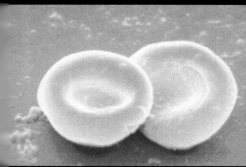

Wrapped in strips of discarded linen sail, the mummy below, undergoing autopsy in a French laboratory, is probably that of a sailor.

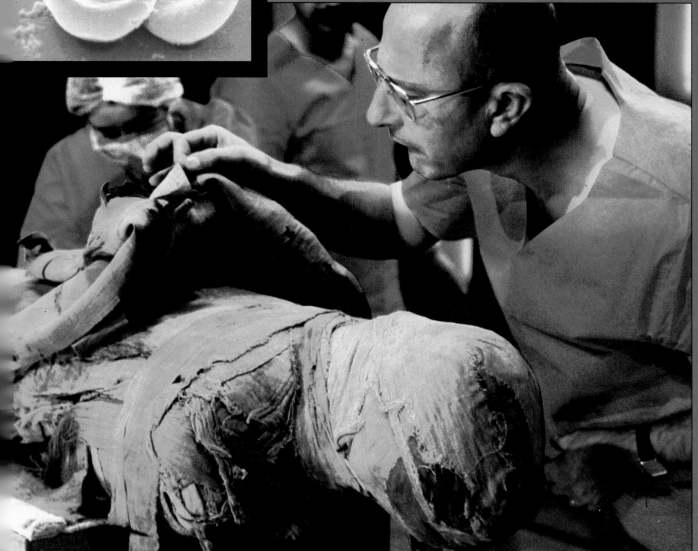

A QUESTION OF MISTAKEN IDENTITY

In their haste to rescue the bodies of the pharaohs and their queens from tomb robbers and transfer them to safety, the ancient priests apparently mislabeled some after they had rewrapped them. Helping to sort out the confusion is the American orthodontist and physical anthropologist James Harris.

Harris, whose lifelong passion has been the study of ancient Egyptians, obtained permission to x-ray the royal mummies in the Cairo Museum. Analysis of the images by Harris and his colleagues enabled them to approximate the ages of the pharaohs at their deaths. When they examined x-rays of a mummy labeled Thutmose I, they discovered the body was that of a 20-year-old, not of the man who, according to historical records, died in his fifties. Here, plainly, was a case of mistaken identity.

Harris x-rayed the skulls of the royal mummies and plotted their bone structure and tooth patterns on a computer. Comparisons demonstrated like features among closely related individuals, but also showed dissimilarities so striking it seemed certain that the priests had mislabeled several of the other royal mummies as well.

In the instance of one unidentified woman, long known to archaeologists only as "the elder lady," Harris produced x-ray evidence *(below)* to show that she might have been none other than Queen Tiy, mother of the heretic pharaoh, Akhenaten.

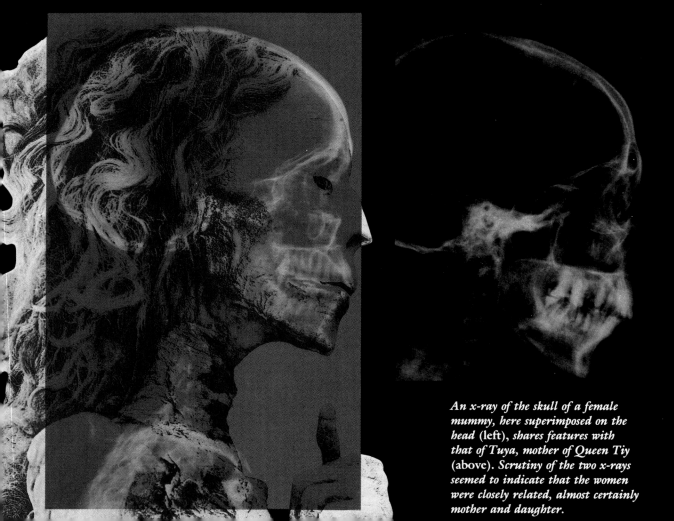

An x-ray of the skull of a female mummy, here superimposed on the head (left), shares features with that of Tuya, mother of Queen Tiy (above). Scrutiny of the two x-rays seemed to indicate that the women were closely related, almost certainly mother and daughter.

A sculptured head of Queen Tiy displays traits matching the mummy at far left. A sample of the mummy's hair matched that of hair from a coffinette (right) associated with Queen Tiy and found in the tomb of Tutankhamen, her reputed grand-son, thus seeming to confirm identification of the body.

RECONSTRUCTING A LIFE

Mummies can shed light on intimate details of the lives of even ordinary people. This proved touchingly so in the case of an anonymous 13-year-old girl, listed only as number 1770 in a Manchester, England, museum.

Her mummy was well over 3,000 years old, but had been rebandaged over a thousand years later, in the fourth century AD, for unknown reasons. When unwrapped in 1975 at the University of Manchester, where it underwent autopsy, the body turned out to be in a poor state, with the skull broken into more than 30 pieces. The teeth were intact, however, and their lack of wear suggested that the girl had survived on a soft or liquid diet. The presence in her intestinal wall of a calcified guinea worm— a debilitating Nile parasite she had probably gotten from her drinking water—doubtless contributed to her condition.

The girl's feet were missing, and both of her legs were broken. Because her flesh showed signs of decomposition, possibly from submersion in water, some think she may have been the victim, not of disease or parasites, but of a Nile crocodile.

To reconstruct the girl's face, clay was applied to a model of the skull (below) in accordance with standard scales of flesh thickness. The parted lips of the finished wax portrait (below, left) *reflect blocked sinuses on the left side of her head, a condition that would have forced the child to breathe through her mouth.*

A LOOK UNDER THE WRAPS

Scientists can now view a mummy without ever unwrapping it or even removing it from its case. They do so by using CAT scanners, machines employed in medicine for making diagnoses without invasive surgery. With scanners they "slice" through the coffin and body in a series of consecutive images. These pictures enable them not only to see whether valuable objects lie concealed within, but also to probe bones and soft tissue for a more complete assessment of ancient ailments than x-raying alone would allow.

Enlisting supercomputers in their probes, scientists take the two-dimensional images produced by CAT scans and turn them into three-dimensional images on their screens. They can then rotate these for viewing the mummy from different angles and, if they wish, manipulate them to depict the subject at various chronological ages.

With the data so obtained, the investigators sometimes go one step further and build up models of the faces of the individuals sealed away in the coffins—adding a new meaning to the ancient notion of an afterlife for the Egyptian dead.

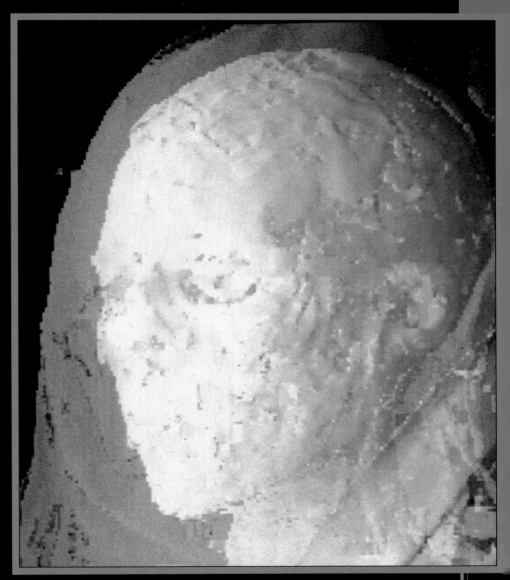

The ghostly face of a wrapped 2,900-year-old mummy of a woman called Tabes emerges from CAT-scan images. Her hair is matted by embalmers' resins, and her nose is pushed out of shape by a funeral mask.

Some mummies speak of ancient violence. Among these is the body of Seqenenre Tao, one of the last rulers of the 17th Dynasty. Seqenenre, a Theban, began the wars that reclaimed the Nile delta and the city of Memphis from the Hyksos, an Asiatic people who had ruled northern Egypt for more than a century. From the struggle would emerge the New Kingdom.

The 30-year-old king below died from head wounds delivered by axes, a mace, and a spear. Some historians have argued that he was assassinated, perhaps as he slept. More recent study indicates otherwise: Seqenenre's wounds, consistent with the bronze weapons used by the enemy, were inflicted in battle.

His death must have been a particularly horrible one. Preliminary healing of bone around the gash at the top of his forehead and contortion of his mummified arm, reflecting paralysis caused by brain damage, are taken as evidence that the king had been initially wounded in an earlier engagement. Despite his weakened condition, he seems to have died fighting a couple of months later; the angle of the gashes suggests that his end came as he was down on his knees. A spear, thrust just behind the king's left ear, probably delivered the fatal wound.

The grimacing head of Seqenenre Tao displays his wounds. Its poorly preserved state is probably due to the king having been hastily embalmed where he fell, so that his body could be sent back to Thebes for a royal burial.

Agony is frozen on the face of an unembalmed body. Bound hand and foot, the anonymous victim had been enclosed in sheepskin—considered ritually unclean by the Egyptians—and placed in a plain coffin for reasons unknown. He was apparently left there to suffocate. The dryness of the tomb dehydrated his body, preserving it.

FOUR

IN
THE
VALLEY
OF
DEATH

The digging would have to stop. For six fruitless seasons George Herbert, fifth earl of Carnarvon, had poured £25,000—the equivalent of more than half a million dollars in today's currency—into the expeditions of the archaeologist Howard Carter in the Valley of the Kings, with little but 13 alabaster pots to show for it. Now, in the summer of 1922, the disappointed aristocrat was ready to abandon the dream they had shared of finding the lost tomb of Tutankhamen. Like a gambler rising from the gaming table after a long losing streak, the earl was drained of desire for further adventure.

Carter, however, was determined to proceed. Facing the total collapse of his lifelong ambition, the short, stocky archaeologist, whose large nose and imperious mustache gave him a fierce expression, boldly asserted that he would carry on at his own expense. Given Carter's financial state, it was probably an empty vow, but Lord Carnarvon was impressed with his friend's conviction and wearily agreed to support one—and only one—more season.

Carter was virtually alone in his belief that Tutankhamen's burial chambers remained intact in the Valley of the Kings. By 1922, his single-minded devotion to his quest had evoked derision from some of his peers. His interest in the tomb had arisen 15 years earlier, in 1907, when a rich American lawyer named Theodore Davis—

An effigy of the deity Anubis, god of embalming and protector of the dead, sits atop the gilded chest on which it rested for 3,245 years in Tutankhamen's tomb, shrouded in a linen shawl (black-and-white photo).

who, in his retirement, had turned to archaeology as a second career—stumbled across a small pit that yielded fragments of artifacts, floral wreaths, and shards of food and wine jars, some of which bore the royal seal of Tutankhamen. As subsequent study revealed, these relics were, in fact, largely refuse from the funerary feast that accompanied the burial of the pharaoh, but Davis claimed that he had located the tomb itself, a conclusion rejected by Carter.

Instead, the discovery of Tutankhamen's seals led Carter to think that the resting place of the young pharaoh would be found near Davis's excavation, in a two-and-a-half-acre triangle of land that encompassed the tombs of three pharaohs—Ramses II, Merenptah, and Ramses VI. His decision to dig only there demonstrated both his resolve and his stubbornness.

Then came the momentous morning of November 4, 1922. As Carter arrived at his latest—and perhaps last—work site, which had been piled with rubble from the tomb of Ramses VI, he was greeted by a strange silence. His laborers had uncovered a step cut into the bedrock and were waiting for him. The archaeologist ordered the excavation to continue immediately and watched, "with ill-suppressed excitement," as a staircase began to appear.

Forming a triumphant party, Lady Evelyn Herbert, her father Lord Carnarvon, Howard Carter, and his assistant, Arthur R. Callendar, pose on the steps to Tutankhamen's tomb shortly after they made one of the century's most spectacular archaeological discoveries.

A linen scarf contains a treasure in gold rings. Found in a box in Tutankhamen's tomb, it had apparently been tossed there by a guard after a robber had tried to make off with the contents. The pharaoh's resting place was burgled at least twice in ancient times, the thieves managing to steal 60 percent of the jewelry.

Sixteen steps led down into a rubble-filled underground passage cut into the rock; it was 27 feet long and took several days to clear. When the tunnel was at last empty, Carter found himself standing before a doorway blocked by large stones that had been plastered over and stamped with the seals of the royal necropolis of the Valley of the Kings. With sinking heart, he could see that the doorway had been penetrated and resealed in ancient times. "Doubts, born of previous disappointments, crept in," he wrote afterward. Was this truly a royal tomb? Had he discovered Tutankhamen at last, only to find his tomb stripped bare by ancient plunderers?

The answers would have to wait another two weeks until his patron—who was in England—could join him. In the meantime, he ordered the tunnel and staircase refilled and topped with boulders, lest modern robbers deprive the two men of the long-dreamed-of experience of opening the tomb themselves.

The Valley of the Kings had been a lure to archaeologists for decades. Although hot, dry, and devoid of almost all living things, it fired the imagination with its awesome history. In this desolate spot in the rocky hills beyond Thebes, 28 mighty pharaohs had been laid to rest in deeply cut tombs that were as much homes as graves, filled with the riches and pleasures of life. The burials were accompanied by dazzling spectacles of wealth and magic. And over the 420 years that the Valley was actively used to house the kings' remains, a thriving community of workers and artisans busied itself carving and decorating the royal tombs, leaving behind an incredible record of their cares and foibles that makes the Valley seem a place not just of the dead, but of the living.

Because of its isolation, the area that was to become known as the Valley of the Kings had seemed safe from tomb robbers, a perfect place for royal burials. Thutmose I (1504-1492 BC), the first pharaoh to be interred here, had chosen it as his final resting place after observing that there was hardly a royal tomb in the whole of Egypt—including the supposedly invulnerable pyramids—that had not been plundered by thieves. Breaking with tradition, he had his tomb hewn from living rock. The interment of his mummy in the Valley set the pattern for three noble dynasties, the 18th, 19th, and 20th. But in time, even the tombs carefully concealed in the cliffs fell prey to robbers. And in Carter's day, archaeologists raced modern thieves for the leavings. More than 50 teams had combed the Valley during the previous 100 years, uncovering most of the burial sites known to exist there. Between 1902 and 1914, the lawyer-excavator Theodore Davis had found no fewer than 30 tombs, all of which had been plundered. "I fear that the valley of the tombs is now exhausted," Davis declared in 1912.

It is not surprising that Carter dissented from this generally accepted verdict. Throughout his career he had followed his own instincts, paying little heed to the opinions of other archaeologists. Trained as a draftsman and watercolorist, he received his first exposure to Egyptology in 1890 at the age of 17, when he was commissioned to do some inking on a set of archaeological tracings. Soon the young artist had gleaned an impressive knowledge, largely self-acquired, of ancient civilizations. While still a teenager, Carter served as an assistant to Flinders Petrie during the archaeologist's excavations of Akhenaten's capital at el Amarna. And he was Davis's first excavation director, participating in the finding of the tomb Queen Hatshepsut built after making herself pharaoh, as well as in the discovery of the treasures of Yuya and Tuya, Queen Tiy's parents.

As his experience grew, Carter was to find an unlikely partner in the elegant and romantic earl of Carnarvon. Nicknamed Lordy by the local Egyptians, Carnarvon was outgoing and genial where Carter was moody and taciturn, but the earl's bluff nature concealed a restless intelligence. Years earlier, a near-fatal automobile accident had shattered his health and left him in constant pain. Advised to take a rest cure, he had traveled to Egypt in 1903. There he developed the passion for Egyptian relics that would give direction to his life.

In 1906, Carnarvon had been financing minor excavations near Luxor when a friend introduced him to Carter. At the time, Carter was scratching out a living as a guide and painting watercolors for tourists, and he eagerly formed an alliance with his wealthy countryman. Their early digs together brought some modest successes, but as Carter's obsession with Tutankhamen deepened, the results grew sparse. Then came that pivotal day when the years of determined digging culminated in what the world was quick to call the most important archaeological find of all time.

With the arrival at Carter's excavation site of Lord Carnarvon, his daughter Lady Evelyn, and their friend Arthur Callendar, Carter

A CROWDED HOME FOR THE YOUNG TUTANKHAMEN

Based on Howard Carter's sketches, as well as on photographs made at the time of discovery, this drawing of Tutankhamen's rock-cut tomb and its contents shows the four rooms as they came to light. From left to right are the antechamber, the so-called annex, the burial chamber, and the treasury.

The enormous shrine around the mummy is cross-sectioned to reveal three interior shrines encasing a massive quartzite sarcophagus in which three coffins nested, the last of pure gold. The adjacent treasury contained, besides the figure of Anubis and the cabinet-like shrine holding the king's em-balmed internal organs, jewel boxes that had been forced open and rifled by robbers.

As he entered the tomb, Carter came first upon the antechamber *(overleaf)*. Dominated by three couches carved in animal shapes, this room was a jumble of precious objects, including chests, chairs, stools, a throne, dismantled chariots, and, in Carter's words, "strange black shrines," out of one of which peeped "a great gilt snake." Two life-size statues of the young pharaoh, each holding a mace and a staff, guarded the door to his resting place.

Carter was bewildered. "The thing was outside all experience," he wrote, "and for the moment it seemed as though there were more to be done than any human agency could accomplish." It took Carter and his helpers seven weeks just to clear the antechamber, and in the process they used over a mile of cotton batting and 32 bales of cheap cotton cloth on the wrapping of objects for transport. All told, they would spend almost a decade emptying the tomb of its more than 3,000 objects, many of which needed on-the-spot conservation.

Reached by a series of 16 steps, Tutankhamen's tomb, hollowed out of limestone, lay 13 feet below ground.

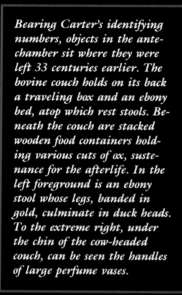

Bearing Carter's identifying numbers, objects in the ante-chamber sit where they were left 33 centuries earlier. The bovine couch holds on its back a traveling box and an ebony bed, atop which rest stools. Beneath the couch are stacked wooden food containers holding various cuts of ox, sustenance for the afterlife. In the left foreground is an ebony stool whose legs, banded in gold, culminate in duck heads. To the extreme right, under the chin of the cow-headed couch, can be seen the handles of large perfume vases.

The gilded wooden statue at left is one of two ka figures of Tutankhamen, made life-size. It is believed that the statues were intended as hiding places for sacred religious texts, but cavities discovered under the kilts—presumably carved to hold the papyri—were empty. The photo above shows Carter and his associate, A. R. Callendar, carefully wrapping one of the figures in February 1923.

THE CURSE THAT WASN'T

"Death comes on wings to he who enters the tomb of a pharaoh," says an Arabic proverb. In 1923 Lord Carnarvon died a few months after entering Tutankhamen's tomb. Sir Arthur Conan Doyle, the creator of Sherlock Holmes, said he believed Carnarvon died as a result of "elementals—not souls, not spirits—created by Tutankhamen's priests" to guard the mummy. Hard-boiled journalists the world over became believers, and in succeeding years the press viewed the demise of anyone involved with Tutankhamen as proof of a curse.

But Carter would have none of this. In his view, "sane people should dismiss such inventions with contempt." Indeed, the doctor on Carter's team who autopsied the body of the king lived for decades afterward to become an octogenarian.

Thanks to Hollywood, the notion of a mummy's curse may still exist; but professional Egyptologists, when asked about it, are likely to say, "Curse? What curse?"

had the refilled passageway cleared and then took up his chisel late on the afternoon of November 26, ready to remove the uppermost blocks in the entryway for a closer look. While these friends watched anxiously over his shoulder, Carter set to work in the dark, cramped passageway. "With trembling hands I made a tiny breach in the upper left-hand corner," he wrote.

Carter slipped his candle through the hole and peered in. "As my eyes grew accustomed to the light," he recalled, "details of the room within emerged slowly from the mist, strange animals, statues, and gold—everywhere the glint of gold. For the moment—an eternity it must have seemed to the others standing by—I was struck dumb with amazement, and when Lord Carnarvon, unable to stand the suspense any longer, inquired anxiously, 'Can you see anything?' it was all I could do to get out the words, 'Yes, wonderful things.'"

Reluctantly, Carter pulled himself away and enlarged the peephole so that all could see. Here before them, untouched for more than 3,000 years, lay a breathtaking array of glittering royal artifacts cramming the small chamber from floor to ceiling.

In writing of these events, Carter relates that he and his companions gazed into the first room, or antechamber, for a time, then carefully sealed up the entryway and withdrew in anticipation of an official opening at a later date, when the Egyptian authorities would be present. His account is commendably consistent with what he should have done according to his agreement with the Egyptian Antiquities Service. But an unpublished narrative, discovered a few years ago among papers in the Metropolitan Museum, records that Carter's party actually spent that entire first night inside the tomb, reveling in their discovery.

By the flickering glow of lanterns, Carter and his companions glimpsed wonders of Egyptian artistry never before seen by modern eyes. Recording in his memoirs his excitement on the occasion of the official opening of the tomb, Carter undoubtedly was describing the furtive delights of that earlier night of exploration.

As Carter began to unlock the secrets of the 3,245-year-old funerary chambers, his attention was drawn to three ceremonial couches dominating one wall of the antechamber. Covered in gold leaf, the furniture had "sides carved in the form of monstrous animals," he wrote. "Uncanny beasts, their heads throwing grotesque shadows on the wall behind them, they were almost terrifying."

More remarkable still, the couches were haphazardly piled

Tutankhamen's throne, made of wood sheathed in gold foil, depicts the queen anointing the king with perfumed ointment. Thieves are thought to have wrenched off and taken the grillwork that once graced the legs; they would have melted down the foil to sell.

with other treasures—alabaster vases, incised boxes and perfume jars, ivory and ebony gaming boards, even a beautifully carved inlaid throne. Everywhere he looked, Carter saw priceless objects that had been roughly handled, probably by thieves who had entered the tomb shortly after Tutankhamen's burial. In a corner of the antechamber lay a jumble of royal chariots, their wooden frames sheathed in gold and encrusted with semiprecious stones.

Beneath one of the couches, Carter spied a small hole—further evidence of tomb robbers—leading into another chamber. This room, thereafter called the annex, was so heaped with riches that not an inch of floor space was left. A quick glance revealed carved stone vessels, inlaid boxes, and elaborately fashioned chairs stacked one on top of the other.

The pharaoh's gilded beds and footstools could be seen upended and scattered throughout both chambers. Reed baskets still contained fruit and bread, and in jugs there were traces of wine—provisions left for the departed ruler to use in the next world. More than 50 chests, some of them decorated with ceremonial, battle, or domestic scenes, contained such items as linens, cosmetics, pendants, and rings. Among the young king's belongings would be found a treasured lock of hair from the head of his grandmother, Queen Tiy, perhaps kept by Tutankhamen as a memento signifying his love for her.

Artifacts of staggering craftsmanship continued to catch the eye, including no fewer than 35 model boats, many of them rigged as if they were about to set sail. A number of these vessels were ritualistic, meant symbolically to ferry the deceased on his journey into the afterlife. Others represented practical, river-going craft fashioned of painted wood.

The most exciting of all these newfound treasures lay ahead. At the far end of the antechamber stood a pair of imposing wooden statues flanking a stone doorway. These statues proved to be life-size portrayals of the king himself, wearing kilts and sandals of shining gold, with linen shawls, frazzled with age, hanging from their shoulders. Their purpose instantly became clear to Carter: The figures were sentinels, left to watch over the remains of the king. "Behind

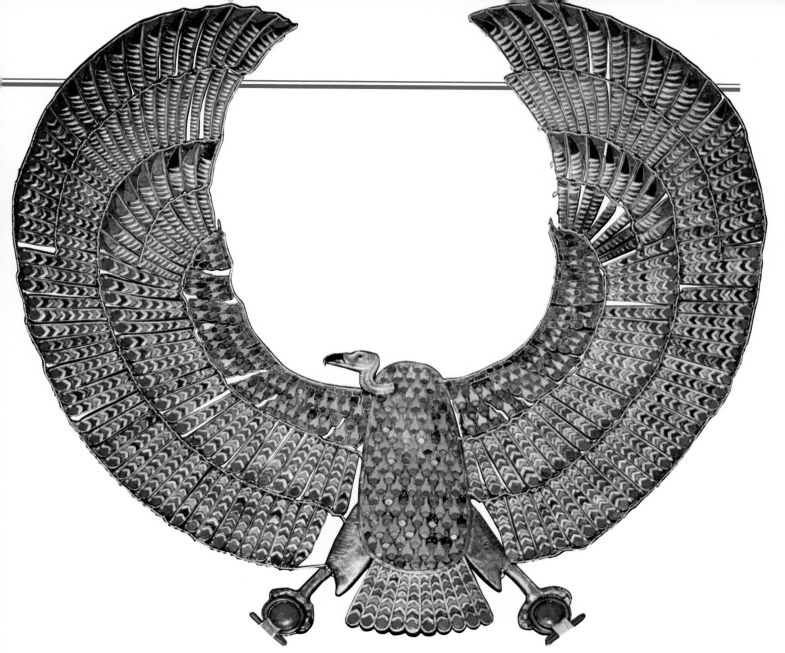

the guarded door," Carter realized, "in all his magnificent panoply of death, we should find the pharaoh lying." Unable to restrain themselves, Carter and his companions slipped into the royal burial chamber that night, using a small hole in the door. Their eyes fell at once on a bedazzling gilded shrine, still bolted. They knew at once that it must contain the mummy of the king.

In a small room entered from the burial chamber, they came upon another glittering shrine, remarkable for the four freestanding carved and gilded figures of goddesses guarding each of its sides. Inside was Tutankhamen's canopic chest, which would not be opened until most of the tomb was cleared years later. Within this translucent block of pristine white calcite Carter would find the internal organs of the departed monarch, contained in four cylindri-

The elaborate flexible golden collar above, which covered the entire chest of Tutankhamen's mummy, depicts the goddess Nekhbet as a vulture. The wings are made of 250 separate segments, and each feather is inlaid with colored glass. The talons clutch the hieroglyph for infinity.

cal chambers sealed with carved stone stoppers, each stopper a small bust of the king. Inside the compartments stood miniature golden coffins—one each for the pharaoh's preserved liver, lungs, intestines, and stomach. Reporting on his experience in the tomb, Carter wrote that he had felt like an intruder in the dust of time.

The archaeologist was overwhelmed. Sorting these treasures would call for the most patient care and planning. Complicating the job was the jumbled state of the tomb's contents, the result of at least two robberies and the hasty efforts of ancient officials to tidy things up afterward. And even in a preliminary examination, it was apparent that many of the artifacts had reached a perilous state of disintegration. A sandal, appearing in sound condition, had crumbled to dust at a slight touch.

During the next few weeks, the Valley of the Kings became a hive of activity: Preservatives and packing materials were brought in, laboratories and darkrooms set up, storerooms readied, and guardhouses constructed. At the same time, Carter enlisted a team of world-renowned experts, including specialists in the conservation of antiquities, scholars of ancient texts, and experienced draftsmen and catalogers. Key among these was the archaeological photographer Harry Burton, on loan from New York's Metropolitan Museum, who recorded on film all the objects found in the tomb, first in the positions they occupied when discovered and then again when removed.

With the influx of scientists and equipment came a stream of journalists. In short order, the discovery of Tutankhamen's tomb became a worldwide sensation, and the Valley soon resembled a bustling fairground. Carter was besieged by reporters and deluged with letters and telegrams. Most correspondents requested souvenirs or offered advice and assistance, but some wrote to warn Carter that he had undoubtedly unleashed a deadly "mummy's curse" when he disturbed the ancient ruler's eternal rest. Hollywood weighed in with a bid for motion-picture rights, and even the clothing industry jumped on the bandwagon with plans for an exclusive line of Tutankhamen-inspired fashions.

While most of the outside world watched in fascination, inside the tomb Carter and his hastily assembled team of experts cleared and cataloged the contents of the densely packed chambers under the watchful eye of Egyptian authorities. It took seven weeks just to clear out the antechamber, and each day brought an increased sense

This gold coffinette, one foot, three-eighths of an inch long, contained Tutankhamen's embalmed intestines.

INSURANCE FOR ETERNITY

To safeguard the dead on their journey into the next life, embalmers tucked a variety of small magic charms known as amulets inside mummy wrappings. Each of the hundreds in use had a special meaning or purpose.

The heart scarab *(right)* was an essential piece symbolizing resurrection and was placed on or in the chest. Shaped like a dung beetle—a creature that seemed to regenerate spontaneously from its own excrement —it bore an inscription to assist wearers as the underworld gods determined their fates. The *djed*-pillar *(left)*, which may have stood for the backbone of Osiris, conferred stability and firmness; the headrest, *weres (right)*, shaped like an Egyptian pillow, signified that the deceased's head would be elevated forever. Most powerful of all amulets was the health-granting Eye of Horus, or *wedjet (below)*. The image represented the eye restored to Horus after he lost it avenging the murder of his father, Osiris.

DJED-PILLAR

HEART SCARAB

HEADREST

EYE OF HORUS

of urgency. Taking down the plaster-covered doorway to the antechamber had broken the tomb's hermetic seal, destroying, after thousands of years, the sterile, stable environment within. James Henry Breasted, an American Egyptologist brought in by Carter, reported hearing "strange rustling, murmuring, whispering sounds," as the objects began to decay at a vastly accelerated rate.

Gradually, the experts drew closer to what Carter called "the decisive moment" of the enterprise—the official opening of the burial chamber. On February 17, 1923, Carter and Lord Carnarvon assembled a small group of scholars and Egyptian officials for the grand unveiling. Lord Carnarvon, according to his brother's memoirs, was as anxious as a "naughty schoolboy," fearful that one of the Egyptian authorities would find evidence of their earlier, unofficial entry.

After a short speech—a bad one, nervously delivered, Carnarvon's brother thought—Carter labored to remove the obstacles that blocked the entrance to the burial chamber. When his guests were allowed in, they stood in respectful silence before an apparent wall of gold—the glittering side of the massive shrine, rather like a modern mausoleum in shape. Pulling back the bolts, Carter opened the door to reveal another gleaming reliquary.

But there was more critical work to be done elsewhere in the tomb, and Carter postponed his examination of the burial chamber until the antechamber could be fully cleared and the objects most in need of immediate preservation attended to. And in the meantime, on April 6, 1923, Lord Carnarvon died after a brief illness, the victim, some claimed, not of pneumonia, but of the supposed mummy's curse *(page 125)*.

It would be almost a year before Carter could open the three remaining shrines. Extraordinary pieces of workmanship, they were nested one within the other and fashioned of gilded wooden panels decorated with scenes of the nether world. Carved on the closed doors to the innermost shrine were two goddesses with wings outspread, as if to protect the body of the king. Slicing through a set of ropes that secured the handles, Carter swung open the doors and exposed a colossal yellow quartzite sarcophagus that, he was relieved to note, was "intact, with its lid still firmly fixed in its place, just as pious hands had left it."

"All we have to do is to peel the shrines like an onion," declared Carter, "and we will be with the king himself." Actually, the task proved considerably more complicated. The outermost of these reliquaries nearly filled the burial chamber, creating cramped working conditions for the excavators. And the narrow spaces between the shrines were crammed with still more artifacts such as wooden staves, ostrich fans, and alabaster urns, including one with a lion artfully carved on top, sticking out a bright red tongue.

Yet another year would elapse before Carter and his assistants could dismantle the heavy shrines and create adequate space in which to examine the sarcophagus. When they had done so, further surprises awaited. The sarcophagus lid, which weighed more than a ton, had apparently been dropped by the ancient workers, leaving a crack running crosswise through its center. The fissure posed a serious problem for the archaeologists. If the broken lid should collapse on top of the contents, the mummy would be destroyed. After considerable debate, Carter's engineers rigged an ingenious set of pulleys to lift the heavy cover safely.

As the lid moved free, it disclosed a large gilded wooden mummy case in the form of the dead pharaoh. The hands were crossed upon the chest, holding the emblems of Egyptian kingship—a flail and a scepter. The face, a remarkable portrait, had been shaped from pure gold with eyes of crystal. This spectacular coffin, however, had apparently been too large to fit inside the sarcophagus. The toes had been filed off, leaving a handful of wooden shavings on the bottom of the coffin.

Fitting snugly within the first coffin lay a second one, even more remarkable, fashioned of gilded wood inlaid with red, blue, and turquoise glass. It was, according to Carter, "the finest example of the ancient coffinmaker's art yet seen." The lid of the second case, in turn, was raised to reveal the third and final coffin, which lay partially obscured in a thin gossamer of linen shrouds and by funerary bouquets left by ancient mourners, the centuries-old leaves and petals looking like last summer's dried flowers. As Carter carefully folded back the delicate fabric, an astounding sight came into view. The innermost coffin was encased in thick gold foil—an "absolutely incredible mass of pure bullion."

Finally, Carter was ready to examine the remains of the king. Slowly, the lid of the golden coffin was raised, exposing the mummy of Tutankhamen swathed in linen bandages and bound by a golden

The gold-bladed dagger above, a superb example of the goldsmith's art, was found tucked into a band around Tutankhamen's waist. The granulated handle is embellished with glass and semiprecious stones.

The calcite lamp at left, shown both unlit and lit, accompanied Tutankhamen to the grave. A burning wick floating on oil made visible a scene showing the king and his wife. When the lamp was discovered, its cup still bore traces of oil.

corselet. Shining brightly against the pale cloth background was a life-size mask of the king, crafted by ancient metalworkers from several sheets of gold. The burnished mask was inlaid with blue glass, quartz, and obsidian, and its chin was adorned with a ceremonial beard. On its brow sat the vulture and cobra, representations of the dieties Nekhbet and Wadjit, the latter poised to spit fire at the pharaoh's enemies.

Thirteen layers of wrappings shrouded the body of the king. Painstakingly, Carter began to slice through the linen with a scalpel. By the thigh, on the right side, a knife had been placed. When pulled from its golden scabbard it proved, surprisingly, to be of iron, possibly made from a meteorite. Its blade, still gleaming like polished steel, was a rare, useful prize for this pre-Iron Age monarch. A golden pectoral hung around the king's throat, signifying the protection of the god Horus. No fewer than 143 pieces of amuletic jewelry lay within the folds of the cloth to ensure the pharaoh's safe transformation from death to immortality.

Despite these careful preparations, time had taken a dreadful toll of the king. The mummy had been liberally doused with resins intended to preserve the flesh. Instead, the liquids had oxidized the body, burning it through a process of self-combustion that left the pharaoh black and shriveled and all but cementing him to the inside of the coffin. Heated knives were required to pry the body—which had to be cut apart—from the coffin. Douglas E. Derry, professor of anatomy at the Egyptian University in Cairo, who assisted Carter, first separated the legs and pelvis from the torso. Then the arms were severed to remove the bracelets decorating them. Finally, the head was taken off so that, with hot knives, it could be removed from the golden mask to which it had adhered. At long last, Carter found himself gazing upon the face of the boy-king. Though the skin was brittle, cracked, and dried to a grayish white pallor, Carter was enthralled with the "well-formed features."

It was February 1932—nearly a decade after he glimpsed that first stone step leading to the tomb—before Carter presented the last of the pharaoh's more than 5,000 precious objects to the Cairo Museum. Although the remains and possessions of Tutankhamen had now been delivered into the modern age, information was sparse about the young pharaoh's life and deeds. His tomb had yielded neither significant inscriptions nor any documents about its occupant. As a result, Tutankhamen's ancestry is still debated, although historians believe that he came to the throne around 1333 BC, at the age of about nine, closely following the reign of the heretical king, Akhenaten.

A stele found at Karnak bears a catalog of Tutankhamen's achievements in righting the damage done by Akhenaten through the imposition of a new state religion: "I found the temples fallen into ruin, with their holy places overthrown, and their courts overgrown with weeds. I reconstructed their sanctuaries, I reendowed the temples, and made them gifts of all precious things. I cast statues of the gods in gold and electrum, decorated with lapis lazuli and fine stones."

Yet Tutankhamen was merely a child when he ascended the throne. His actions doubtless were controlled by advisers—particularly the powerful Ay, who was possibly the father of Nefertiti, and the general Horemheb, both of whom would eventually assume the throne themselves. A number of objects from the tomb show a warlike Tutankhamen in battle, subduing his enemies, but these representations may have been more symbolic than real. An inscription in the tomb of Horemheb at Memphis, however, does support the picture of the young pharaoh at war. It records Horemheb as having been "in attendance on his lord upon the battlefield on this day of smiting the Asiatics."

The young king's early passing created a brief but remarkable power struggle in Thebes. He and his queen Ankhesenamen had failed to produce an heir, despite the sad evidence of their attempts—two tiny mummified fetuses, buried with the pharaoh. Shortly after her husband's death, his young widow, sensing enemies around her, begged Suppi-

NOTEPADS OF DISCARDED STONE

Making use of a by-product of their industry, the artists and workers of Deir el Medina often drew or wrote on hand-size limestone flakes, or ostraca, that accumulated as carvers chiseled tombs from the rock. On the chips' clean white surfaces they scribbled letters, kept accounts, and made notes, drawings of projects, or cartoons to amuse their colleagues, all of which provide insights into the lives and humor of the village's talented inhabitants.

The sketch above is a plan of the tomb of Ramses IX. The drawings below depict two boys burnishing a jar, a cat shepherding geese, and a caricature of a stonemason. The round head, bulbous nose, open mouth, big ears, and unshaven jowls create the cartoon image of a simpleton.

The ruins of Deir el Medina, the walled village of the Valley of the Kings' tomb makers and associated artisans, include numerous house sites whose owners' names are known to history. One inhabitant used the brush and stool above when dusting off the lower portion of limestone tomb walls before the surfaces were painted.

luliumas, the king of the Hittites, to send her one of his sons to be her spouse and share the throne of Egypt. "If thou wouldst give me one son of thine," she wrote to Suppiluliumas, "he would become my husband. Never shall I pick out a servant of mine and make him my husband. I am afraid!"

After secret negotiations, a Hittite prince was duly sent. But the prospective bridegroom disappeared before reaching Egypt, possibly the victim of assassins. Whatever her misgivings, it is believed the queen yielded to necessity and accepted her ambitious grandfather, Ay, some 40 years her senior, as husband.

The mystery deepened when Tutankhamen's remains were reexamined by British doctors in 1968. It had originally been thought that the pharaoh died of tuberculosis, but x-rays of his skull suggest cranial damage consistent with a sharp blow to the head. The new evidence points to a possible chariot accident or even murder, perhaps at the instigation of an aging Ay, impatient for the throne.

During his four-year reign, Ay eradicated inscriptions honoring Tutankhamen, replacing them with ones glorifying himself, and, within a few generations, the boy-king's name was routinely omitted from the official lists of Egypt's rulers, just as Akhenaten's was. But in an ironic twist of history, it is Tutankhamen who has become celebrated around the world. The young pharaoh's tomb may have been a small one, but he and his family had at their command the wealth of the greatest period of Egyptian history. Experts, therefore, do not believe that larger tombs before or after were necessarily filled with a greater variety of goods or richer artifacts than were found in Tutankhamen's chambers. A careful study of these objects could offer fresh insights into Egyptian life, yet most of them have never been the subject of serious scholarly examination.

Artifacts and relics may have much to say, but they cannot substitute fully for the written word. Historians, ironically, know more about the men who carved the burial chambers of kings like Tutankhamen than they do about many of the men put to rest in them. In a strange archaeological paradox, the residents of the small village of Deir el Medina have left the far richer record.

Deir el Medina was founded during the rule of Thutmose I. Having chosen to conceal his final resting place in the Valley of the Kings, the pharaoh needed to create a village of workers to build his tomb. To preserve the secrecy of the tomb's whereabouts, the town itself had to be isolated, a complete world unto itself. The king accomplished this by building the village in a well-concealed valley and surrounding it with a brick wall, thereby establishing his own private colony of royal tomb artisans. Generation after generation of workmen lived within this enclosed hamlet, passing their skills from father to son as they labored to create monuments worthy of each reigning pharaoh.

Digging amid the village's ruins, archaeologists have recovered thousands of limestone flakes and potsherds known as ostraca, upon which the residents of Deir el Medina doodled, sketched, and scribbled messages. The largest deposit of ostraca came from a single pit excavated between 1948 and 1950 by the French archaeologist Bernard Bruyère. These fragments, which were used like scrap paper by the Egyptians, proved to be letters, receipts, work records, lawsuits, laundry lists, even magical spells to ward off illness. Based on information gleaned from ostraca, modern researchers have built a portrait, in surprisingly intimate detail, of how this singular group of Egyptians lived.

Today, visitors can view the ruins of Deir el Medina and imagine the bustling hamlet that once thrived there, even stopping to

LIFESTYLE OF AN AFFLUENT COUPLE

Almost all the tombs of ancient Egypt have been plundered, but one was somehow overlooked—and a good thing it was. It yielded an extraordinary inventory of items—including even a toilet—that shows how the well-to-do lived 3,500 years ago. The tomb, belonging to a man called Kha and his wife Merit, was discovered in 1906 by the Italian archaeologist Ernesto Schiaparelli, whose workers are seen here with the couple's possessions.

Kha was a self-made man who was able to win the esteem of King Thutmose III and become his superintendent of public works at Deir el Medina. X-rays of his mummy show him wearing a gold coiled necklace, a royal gift. But although Kha was advanced in years when he died, his tomb effigy depicts him as a young man (right), garlanded with withered flowers. Like this wreath, the other items in the tomb were in an excellent state of preservation.

TOOLS OF A BUILDER'S TRADE

BALANCE CASE

In charge of construction in the Theban area during the reign of Thutmose III, Kha continued in his post under Amenhotep II. Tools were thus important to him. Among those buried with him was a wooden case *(above)* that had once held a bronze balance consisting of a rod from which weighing pans could be suspended. The pans were kept in the circular section, the beam in the rectangular portion.

The tomb also contained an adz for planing timber and a drill, rotated by moving a bow whose string was wrapped around the drill handle. Perhaps the most important tools of Kha's officialdom were his wooden tablet and ink palette for making calculations and writing memos. Coated with wax, the tablet could be wiped clean and reused. But certainly Kha's most cherished tool must have been his gilded cubit measure, or ruler, about 21 inches long, awarded to him by Amenhotep II for his swift completion of a building.

ADZ

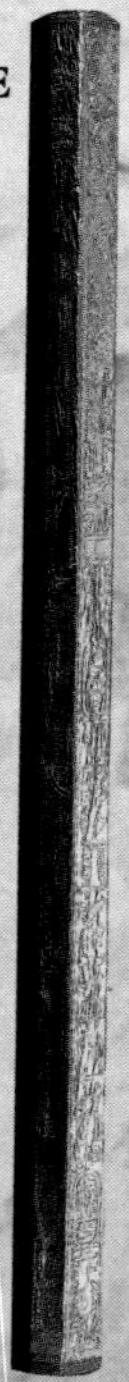

CUBIT MEASURE

DRILL

THE TRAPPINGS OF ELEGANCE

Like most Egyptians, Kha and Merit took pride in their grooming and clothing. Each of Kha's 17 tunics, 50 loincloths, and 26 shirts was monogrammed. His winter-weight linen tunic—shown against a backdrop of the rock-cut tomb—had tapestry bands. As a further indication of his fastidiousness, Kha used a bronze razor and horse-shaped tweezers *(far right)* to remove unwanted facial and body hair, as was the Egyptian custom.

Merit's wig, found still on its stand, was made of human hair, which she may have dressed with pins and a comb. In her wooden cosmetic chest she kept glass and alabaster jars filled with scented oils and creams, and kohl, an eye paint also used in eye medicines. While accenting Merit's eyes, the dark paste may have cut down on the sun's glare.

TABLET AND PALETTE

HAIR ACCESSORIES

WIG

TUNIC

RAZOR

TWEEZERS

COSMETIC BOX

BED

RUG

TOILET

DELIGHTS AND COMFORTS OF A WELL-FURNISHED HOME

Kha's and Merit's furnishings—some of which are superimposed here over a photo of the tomb's crowded main chamber—suggest that the couple's home was indeed a cozy one. At the end of the day, they could relax barefoot over a game of senet *(right)*, displayed atop a faux-reed table. They may have rested their feet on the lotus-patterned rug with tufted center and fringed and knotted edges *(far left)*. Bedtime offered warmth against the cold desert night with covers of woven pile like those spread on Merit's bed *(left)* in one of Schiaparelli's photographs; beneath these, layers of linen fabrics rested on a spring of braided cord neatly strung across the bedframe. Since the foot end of beds almost always sloped downward in ancient Egypt, a footboard was needed. And if in the night Kha or Merit responded to a call of nature, a stool, made into a toilet *(bottom left)*, was at hand. A pan of sand placed underneath would be emptied by servants in the morning.

GAME AND TABLE

inspect the ruins where, some 30 centuries earlier, the dwelling of a particular coppersmith or stonemason once stood.

Contrary to popular belief, the royal tomb artisans were not slave laborers but highly skilled artisans. They lived with their families in mudbrick houses with flat roofs made of wood beams and matting. As many as 70 houses stood in rows along narrow, alleylike streets. Many households were quite large, with 15 children noted in some cases, and pets such as cats, monkeys, baboons, and gazelles common. Laundresses were supplied by the government to wash the inhabitants' clothes, and servant girls to grind their grain.

The wives of the workmen cared for their many children, baked bread, and wove clothing. Under Egyptian law, these women of long ago had property rights more advanced than those of the wives of the American and British archaeologists studying them. They held title to their own wealth and to a third of all marital goods. This portion would belong solely to the wife in case of divorce or on her husband's death; if she died first, it would go, not to her spouse, but to her heirs.

Serving as intermediaries between the pharaoh's authorities and the villagers were two foremen and a scribe, acknowledged as the town's leaders. Together with their deputies and other town notables they constituted a court, which tried civil and criminal cases. Lively lawsuits were brought by the townspeople, each of whom conducted his or her own case.

Leaving their village homes, the craftsmen would file through the single gateway in the wall and march off for a prescribed period of labor at the latest tomb site. There they lived in small stone huts for eight days, after which they got two days off to go home. As each laborer reported to the tomb, his arrival was noted by the scribe on an attendance sheet, like a modern factory worker's timecard. Occasionally an artisan would miss work, and then as now the excuses

Tools of the tomb painter's trade, the rope brush was used for covering large wall areas, and the basalt tray for holding unground pigments. Draftsmen sketched outlines in red; supervisors corrected the designs in black. Then artists went to work, filling in the blanks with pure yellow, green, red, blue, black, or white.

MYSTERY MUMMY IN A MYSTERY TOMB

Archaeology in the Valley of the Kings has taken a new twist—the reexamination of sites unearthed years ago. Among those working there now is Donald P. Ryan, an American who in 1989 rediscovered tomb KV60. (All the tombs are numbered, with KV shorthand for "Kings' Valley.") KV60 had been opened in 1903 by Howard Carter, who found two female mummies, only one of which was in a coffin. Apparently finding it uninteresting, he closed the tomb and left no map of its exact location. In 1906 another archaeologist happened on it and had the mummy in the coffin shipped to the Cairo Museum, where the body was identified as that of the nurse of Queen Hatshepsut, the famous female pharaoh, whose own remains have never been found.

When Ryan reopened KV60, he found lying on the floor the abandoned mummy—that of an elderly female whose shrunken, folded flesh suggested that she had been obese in life and whose nails were painted red, outlined in black. Her left arm, with clenched fist, lay diagonally across her chest, a pose thought to have been reserved for female royalty of the 18th Dynasty. Ryan also found a fragment of a wooden face piece from a coffin lid, with a notched chin where a false beard—a male emblem—may have been attached.

Who is the mysterious regal woman, and why was she not in a coffin? Why would a male coffin turn up in a tomb for two women? Ryan is unable to supply answers but hopes that in time new finds in the Valley will illuminate the mystery.

could be quite inventive. "Eye trouble" and "brewing beer" were popular alibis. One craftsman, Hechnekhu, perhaps having exhausted more traditional pretexts, provided a memorable reason for his absence: He could not come to work because he was busy embalming his mother.

Working two four-hour shifts each day, the stonemasons would cut into the living rock with stone, copper, or bronze chisels pounded with heavy wooden mallets. A team of plasterers followed, coating the walls with a layer of gypsum and whitewash to make them as smooth as possible. The dressed walls would then be turned over to draftsmen, who would carefully sketch out texts and designs, which sculptors, using bronze chisels, would painstakingly carve into reliefs. The reliefs were painted with pigments made from minerals such as carbon, ocher, iron oxide, azurite, and malachite.

Daylight did not penetrate the inner chambers of the vaults, so the crews developed an effective means of artificial lighting. Pieces of linen, treated with oil or fat, were twisted into wicks, which would burn brightly. Salt applied to the wicks reduced excessive smoke that might have damaged the reliefs.

Most of the toilers appear to have been conscientious, and for their efforts were paid in rations of emmer wheat and barley, which were used to make bread and beer (the beer was more like a slurry than the effervescent beverage of today). Every so often the laborers received a bonus, which could take the form of sesame oil, blocks of salt, or—most highly prized of all—meat, usually that of an ox. Despite the orderly structure of the work force, not everything ran smoothly in Deir el Medina. The delivery of food and supplies sometimes proved unreliable, prompting bitter complaints to the vizier, the pharaoh's chief administrative official, who appeared often to inspect the work sites. Disgruntled artisans frequently complained about pay and conditions. "I am to you like the donkey," groused one draftsman to his superior. "If there is some work, bring the donkey. If there is some beer, you do not look for me, but if there is work, you do look for me. I am a man who has no beer in his house. I try to fill my belly by writing to you."

A foreman named Paneb during the reign of Ramses II developed a particular antipathy for his vizier. By all accounts, Paneb was a bit of a rogue; when he was not quarreling with his co-workers, he was pursuing their wives. And he had faced a charge not unknown in the modern world: He used government equipment and employees for his own private work. Paneb was equally aggressive in seeking his rights. When his grievances drew no action from the vizier, he took the remarkable step of complaining directly to the pharaoh himself. Paneb evidently found the king in a sympathetic mood, for the vizier was relieved of his duties.

Not all the pharaohs were as receptive as Ramses II. On November 14, 1165 BC, during the reign of Ramses III, the laborers of Deir el Medina became so exasperated by delays of supplies that they threw down their tools and marched off the job. Gathering together, the workmen staged what may have been the first sit-down strike in history. Village leaders attempted to reason with them but were met, according to the scribe Amennakht, with "great oaths."

"It is because of hunger and thirst that we came here," declared one of the strikers. "There is no clothing, no fat, no fish, no vegetables. Send to Pharaoh our good Lord about it, and send to the vizier our superior, that we may be provided for." Once the workers' grievances were reported to the authorities, they received the long-delayed rations. The next morning the men were back on the job.

The artisans of Deir el Medina displayed, in their writings and achievements, an enormous vitality that seems at odds with their preoccupation with death and the afterlife. Yet this may not be as paradoxical as it appears, for the powerful religious assertion that you *can* take it with you meant to the Egyptians that accomplishments

FATEFUL DATE WITH GODS OF THE DEAD

The Egyptians believed that a glorious afterlife awaited those who truly deserved it. They envisioned a divine committee judging souls before allowing them entry into Duat, the land of the justified dead. Anubis, protector of mummies, placed the heart of the deceased on scales and weighed it against a feather worn in the headdress of Maat, goddess of order. Thoth, wise and honest scribe of the gods, recorded the good and bad the heart contained. Those whose hearts balanced perfectly with the feather won eternal life; the rejected were devoured by Ammit, monster of the dead.

Once admitted to the underworld, the newcomers could expect the protection of several deities. Chief among these was Osiris, who, according to myth, had

reigned as an early king of Egypt before being hacked to pieces by his jealous brother, Seth. After the devoted Isis, Osiris's wife and sister, reassembled his body, he was resurrected as Duat's supreme governor. Pharaohs—who in life were the living embodiment of Horus, Osiris's son—were believed to become Osiris with their passing, a privilege that, as Egypt grew more democratic in the Middle Kingdom, fell to anyone who led a moral life.

In this wall painting from the tomb of Thutmose IV, the dead pharaoh meets Osiris (far left), then proceeds to the jackal-headed Anubis and on to Hathor, each of whom presents him with an ankh, the symbol of life. Hathor, who conducted the deceased along the dangerous paths to the land of the dead, is seen here twice, wearing her traditional headdress of cow horns bracketing the sun.

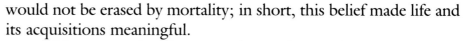

would not be erased by mortality; in short, this belief made life and its acquisitions meaningful.

The spectacle of a properly conducted funeral, especially when carried out with the pomp accorded royalty, must have come as a kind of special reward for the workers of Deir el Medina after devoting years of their lives to the carving and decorating of a tomb. Few funerals could have been more stirring than that of the great pharaoh Ramses II, who died around 1224 BC after reigning almost 67 years. His splendid achievements suggest the heights Tutankhamen might have reached had he lived longer. Ramses brought his empire into a period of renewed prosperity and peace. A fierce warrior, he had repeatedly campaigned against Egypt's enemies with his highly trained army of charioteers, archers, and foot soldiers. Over a lifetime, he sired at least 90 children, surviving 12 of his male offspring. A tireless builder of monuments, he left more tributes to himself than any other pharaoh. Some of these, however, were stolen credits, acquired by chiseling from established monuments the identities of their builders and substituting his own name.

After such a long and prosperous reign, which was almost twice as long as most Egyptians' lifetimes, Ramses' death must have called for the scrupulous observation of the funerary rituals to guarantee the quick passage of the deceased to his place among the gods. Pictures of the great pharaoh's tomb, explored in 1913 by the photographer-archaeologist Harry Burton but today closed to the public, show what a lavish underground palace it was, compared with Tutankhamen's small tomb. The entry corridor alone descends more than 150 feet below the surface of the Valley, and the burial chamber has nearly 2,000 square feet of floor space and an arched roof more than 23 feet high.

Although no written records of Ramses' funeral exist, scholars are able to reconstruct what the ceremony must have been like from elaborate depictions of rites carved on the walls of kings' burial chambers and set out in the Book of the Dead, a collection of funerary spells and rituals displayed in most royal tombs. Following the traditional 70-day ritual of embalming in the pharaoh's new capital of Pi-Ramses, which lay

143

400 miles north of the Valley in the Nile delta, the mummified body of Ramses would have been set aboard the lead vessel of a flotilla and conveyed up the Nile to Thebes, the old religious center. Ramses' successor, 60-year-old Merenptah, would follow on the royal barge, while the common people lined the riverbanks to watch the procession and mourn the king's death. Merenptah was required to take an active role in the funeral, since the Egyptians believed that only by seeing the burial rituals to their successful conclusion did the presumed successor establish his legitimacy as heir.

On landing in Thebes, the mummy would be placed upon an ox-drawn sledge for the procession to the tomb. Led by shaven-headed priests chanting and wafting incense, the funeral train would wend its way into the Valley, its ranks swelled by professional mourners and servants carrying royal possessions. Two women impersonating Isis and Nephthys, the goddesses who were the chief mythic mourners at ancient Egyptian funerals, would follow. At the entrance of the tomb, the royal bier would be greeted by ritual dancers, and by a priest who read funerary spells from a section of papyrus. Then would come the most important ceremony of the entire proceeding, the symbolic rite of Opening the Mouth, supervised by Merenptah himself. The ritual's purpose was to bestow upon the mummy the powers of speech, sight, and hearing, restoring it to life for its existence in the beyond. The body, in its humanoid coffin, was placed upright before the entrance to the tomb by a priest wearing a mask of the jackal-headed god Anubis. Two other priests would ceremoniously touch the mouth of the mummy with an array of magical and amuletic objects such as the ankh, the ancient symbol of life.

This ritual completed, the departed pharaoh would receive offerings of clothing, incense, and food. The mourners, in turn, would partake of a funerary banquet. At the end of the festivities, the mummy was conveyed into the tomb and installed in the burial chamber. The footprints of the funeral party would be swept from the floor. Then the door to the tomb would be blocked with masonry, sealed, and covered with rubble, presumably closed forever.

Forever, however, in the case of Ramses' tomb, was not to be.

Today it lies in a shocking state of ruin, its limestone walls damp and cracked, tons of flash-flood debris clogging its ancient passages. With each passing year, as moisture causes swelling of the shale layer underneath, the tomb of Ramses II draws closer to total destruction.

The Valley of the Kings remains an unfinished puzzle. A pharaoh here, a queen, prince, or high priest there, are unaccounted for. And the possibility of a major find—perhaps even one to rival Carter's—is never farther than the next unexplored tomb. Somewhere in the Valley there is, probably, at least one pharaoh's tomb that has never been located—that of Ramses VIII. Like Tutankhamen, this king reigned a short time, only five years (1136-1131 BC). No stele recites his accomplishments, nor has reference to him been noted anywhere except in a list of princes, offspring of Ramses III, carved on a wall of his funerary temple at Medinet Habu in western Thebes. Ramses VIII's tomb has eluded resolute modern seekers, and so, perhaps, it may also have escaped the ancient plunderers.

A few noblemen, priests, and other commoners were interred in the Valley of the Kings. Believed by some scholars to be there, but currently unaccounted for, is the tomb of Herihor. Although not a pharaoh, he was an important figure in the reign of Ramses XI. An army officer who became a high priest, he forged an unusual combination

A cutaway of the decorated tomb of Seti I, painted by its 19th-century discoverer, Giovanni Battista Belzoni, shows the sloping 328-foot-long passage leading to the burial chamber. Considered the greatest of the New Kingdom tombs, it is decorated throughout with wall reliefs and paintings. The pit may have been designed to impede or trap robbers.

145

of careers that set him at the pinnacle of power and wealth, a status that his tomb and its contents might well reflect.

Tombs that were long ago explored can still yield treasures. Many early excavators dug narrow tunnels through the rubble, removed the most easily grasped or most artistically interesting objects and moved on, leaving a great deal behind. Recently, for example, in the tomb of Ramses VI, through which thousands of people shuffle daily, an archaeologist casually picked at a shallow hole in a corner of one of the chambers and found a statuette of the pharaoh. And in some of these tombs, periodical flash flooding through the ages has buried, but preserved rather than damaged, ancient remains. The rainwaters have washed in, then drained away quickly after depositing fine silt that has formed a cementlike barrier against oxygen, bacteria, and other agents of decay. Much of value may yet be found in the overlooked debris of tombs excavated hastily—and superficially—in years past.

Even the most prominent and visited of tombs may still have objects of value to yield. Beneath the floor of what has been assumed to be the burial chamber in the tomb of Seti I is a stairway leading down to a long, rubble-clogged passageway. Giovanni Battista Belzoni, the tomb's discoverer, crawled 300 feet through this tunnel until he was stopped by a wall of debris. No one has gone beyond that impediment. There are several theories about the passageway, including that of the American archaeologist Kent R. Weeks, who recently followed Belzoni's route through the tunnel. Weeks speculates that at its end may be found the real burial chamber, the other having been put there to fool thieves. A sarcophagus found by Belzoni in one of the supposed burial chamber's rooms could have belonged to a member of the pharaoh's family, rather than to the pharaoh himself; other tombs, such as that of Merenptah, Ramses II's successor, apparently have held two sarcophagi. And the mummy of Seti was found not in his tomb but in the famous cache of 1881, where it had been hidden away by ancient priests eager to save the remains of pharaohs whose tombs were being desecrated by robbers.

In 1986, Weeks began probing a tomb whose entrance had been observed a century before but was later concealed by rubble. Weeks believed that the tomb, which was known only as KV5, might lie near the entrance to the Valley of the Kings, perhaps under the parking lot used by tourist buses. There, in the vicinity of the tomb of Ramses II, Egyptologists had speculated that some of the princes

In an effort to save the Valley of the Queens' most beautiful tomb, that of Queen Nefertari, an Italian team of restorers works on the flaking murals. Begun in 1986, the six-year endeavor was sponsored by the Egyptian Antiquities Organization and the J. Paul Getty Conservation Institute.

146

sired by the prolific pharaoh might be buried. Weeks called in Vincent Murphy, a Massachusetts geophysicist skilled in subsurface exploration, to help find the tomb.

Murphy, sponsored by the New York financier Bruce Heafitz, brought to Egypt three types of electronic sensors to penetrate the land surface and reveal any secrets it might conceal. One was a low-frequency radar that sends signals into the ground, charting the echoes as they bounce back. These returning impulses vary, depending on whether they are passing through layers of sand, clay, or rock, and also with the depth of each layer. The second sensor was a seismic device like those used in assessing earthquakes. Both of these instruments had been used successfully in other archaeological locations, but only the third type—a magnetometer—proved effective here, in the dry limestone cliffs of the Valley of the Kings. This sensitive, hand-held instrument reacts to changes in the earth's magnetic field. All rocks are slightly magnetic, so the magnetometer can measure their magnetism and provide a "thumbprint" for a given site. A gap in the rocks left by a tomb entrance provides a different magnetic configuration from that of an unbroken rock formation. Murphy took readings from known tomb entrances, then combed the area with his magnetometer to find a similar thumbprint.

After two days of probing, Murphy established a perimeter of approximately one-eighth of an acre. And indeed within this space the entrance to a tomb was found just 150 feet from the spacious burial complex of Ramses II—under the parking lot. The entry-chamber walls verified that some of Ramses' sons had indeed been interred there. The magnetometer had located the long-lost tomb, but it took traditional methods—and insight—to get the excavation under way, especially since the chambers had been filled practically to the ceiling with silt from flash floods.

It was fortunate that the tomb was rediscovered, for it had suffered serious damage to its entry chambers since the 1960s when sewer and water lines were laid over the hidden vault, and further delays would have ruined more of the plaster reliefs that were already falling off the walls. One of the pipes from the Valley of the Kings Resthouse—a coffee shop originally built for the tourists that had flocked to Tutankhamen's crypt after its discovery—had been leaking sewage into the tomb for 20 years.

A line from the Book of the Dead on the walls of Tutankhamen's innermost shrine reads, "I am yesterday, I know tomorrow." The discovery, in archaeology's infancy, of the boy-king's bountiful tomb holds out the hope of finding another one, still intact, perhaps tomorrow. If such a site exists in the Valley of the Kings, the use of electronic sensors enhances the possibility of its discovery. But these devices only show anomalies in the ground. They may beep at the presence of a tomb's doorway, but the particular qualities of a Carter—audacity, stubbornness, creativity, and insights honed by training and experience—will still be required to spawn tomorrow's great Egyptian finds.

THE PERSONAL TUTANKHAMEN

Jeweled, robed, and seated on his child-size throne, his small hands grasping the royal crook and flail, Tutankhamen would have inspired awe among his bowing subjects even as a nine-year-old, his age on becoming pharaoh. But out of the public gaze and in the cloistered world of his family, the god-king would simply have been a boy, playing games with his sisters or learning to read and write; and later, an adolescent absorbed in clothes, sports, and love.

Although his parentage is uncertain, Tutankhamen is thought to have been the son of the pharaoh Akhenaten and Kiya, a minor queen. His child's features appear in the wooden head above, portraying him as the infant sun god Re at birth, rising from a blue lotus. Examination of his mummy revealed that, as a young adult, he was small-boned and five feet five inches tall.

The king's slight frame cannot be attributed to poor nutrition. The contents of his tomb reflect a nourishing diet consisting of breads and cakes made of wheat and barley, and protein-rich foods such as beef shoulder and sheep ribs, seasoned with spices and sweetened with honey. For dessert there were dates, figs, grapes, almonds, and fruits of palm. Perhaps he snacked on watermelon seeds; 11 baskets of them were found. And he was amply provided in the afterlife with at least 30 large jars of vintage wine.

Tutankhamen's reign was dominated by powerful adults demanding his acquiescence in schemes for reviving the old gods that had been cast aside by Akhenaten in favor of one divinity, the Aten. At age 18 he died. Some evidence of a blow to his skull has led to the suggestion that his death resulted from an accident; it has also engendered speculation that he was murdered.

Upon the opening of Tutankhamen's tomb more than three millennia later, his cherished belongings were photographed one at a time (all the black-and-white pictures on these pages come from that record). Instead of scrolls proclaiming mighty deeds, there were artfully rendered scenes of domestic bliss and leisure-time pursuits. Bared were the mundane details of his existence; amid elaborate finery lay abundant stores of the young pharaoh's underwear.

THE CHILD-KING AT STUDY AND PLAY

The attractive youngster whose cherubic features are cast in gold at right must have charmed his doting relatives. It is easy to visualize Tutankhamen's small figure scampering along the garden paths of the North Riverside Palace in Akhetaten, the capital, or absorbed in the ancient board game of senet. He would continue, as an adult, to play such games, four of which accompanied him into his tomb.

No record of his boyhood academic achievements has been left, but he probably began his education at four as did other wellborn Egyptian children, learning first to read, then to write. A great quantity of scribal equipment was placed in his tomb. In the afterlife, his people believed, a pharaoh serves as a scribe to the sun god.

The king's name decorates the oval box below. The three hieroglyphs at the top, making up the name of the god Amen, are placed in the most important position. The bird flanked by bread loaves reads *tut*, and to its left is *ankh*, for "life." On the last row, the crook, translating as "ruler," is accompanied by two signs representing the city of Thebes.

The gold earrings below, found in the box at left and showing signs of wear, adorned the king in childhood, as was customary among Egyptian males of his time. Ear holes can be seen in the carved figure of the pharaoh (right).

Inlaid with ivory geometric designs across its back, the child-size ebony chair below is similar in style to the king's adult throne. It rests on ivory-clawed lion's paws. Panels of gold leaf on the sides portray plants and an ibex at rest.

On state occasions, the boy-king held a small crook and flail, signifying divine rule. The flail's base bears the early form of his name, Tutankhaten, suggesting that this may have been the flail he held at his coronation. It was found in the box shown here, with the archaeologists' markers in place.

SPORTS OF A ROYAL ADOLESCENT

Tutankhamen's adolescent pursuits are variations of those familiar to teenagers today: He collected one-of-a-kind items, loved to drive his chariots, and, despite his apparently frail physique, entered enthusiastically into sports such as swimming, fishing, and hunting. In addition to pursuing waterfowl, hare, gazelle, ibex, antelope, and ostrich, he may even have gone after the powerful and dangerous hippopotamus.

As a child, Tutankhamen had practiced for hunting and warfare with a miniature, foot-long bow. By the time of his death, the king had acquired 46 bows, the largest of which measured six feet. Nearly 400 arrows were buried with him along with a multitude of clubs, boomerangs, and knives. Six chariots also accompanied him into his tomb; four of them were state vehicles, built of wood overlaid with gilt and decorated with reliefs and glass inlays. The two lightest were especially suitable for swift maneuvering during hunting.

A cane ornamented with two captives, a Nubian and an Asian bound together *(below)*, was one of some 130 walking sticks deposited in the king's tomb, each different from the other. Tutankhamen may well have collected them as a hobby. Amid staves of ebony, ivory, silver, and gold was one simple reed. It suggests that while strolling along the Nile one day, the boy-king decided to make a stick for himself. Banded with gold at the top and bottom, the staff bears a proud inscription: "A reed that his majesty cut with his own hand."

Fanned by servants as he rides in his chariot, the king vanquishes his Nubian enemies (above). The scene, considered by some to be more symbolic than realistic, was painted on a chest found in the antechamber (below, left).

These ivory boomerangs may have been used for hunting fowl. But they had another function as well: In the afterlife, they could be hurled at birds of evil.

Discovered wrapped in linen, a gilded statue shows the king as the god Horus (right) slaying the god Seth, depicted as a hippopotamus. A real hunter of that era would perch on his papyrus boat and harpoon the hippo, then drag the animal to shore for the kill.

This gold fan tells its own tale in the embossed picture. While hunting, the king had obtained the ostrich feathers that once decorated the fan's edge.

PHARAOH IN HIS DRESSING ROOM

The dressing of the pharaoh was a ritual event carried out in front of favored courtiers. That Tutankhamen was well equipped to fulfill this duty is attested to by a profusion of items from the tomb—clothing, sandals, necklaces, jewels, a pair of mirror boxes, and a life-size wooden mannequin bearing the king's visage *(opposite)*, cut off at the hips and above the elbows. Its body was painted white to imitate a shirt and was probably used for displaying robes or elaborate jeweled collars.

Under his customary knee-length kilt, the pharaoh wore a triangular linen loincloth *(bottom right)*, tied around the waist. More than a hundred of these were found, all neatly bundled, some paired with kilts. The standard kilt consisted of a rectangle of linen wrapped around the waist, fastened in front with the long overlapping end arranged in pleats.

Sometimes the king wore undershirts, which were adorned with embroidery at the neckline. Even such simple garments represented a significant investment of labor; the making of one of his childhood shirts, by some estimates, took 3,000 hours.

Gloves were rare and were worn only by the upper class. Tutankhamen's 27 pairs amazed modern glovemakers, for they were sewn with a stitch unknown until it was reinvented in the 18th century. The child's glove of fine linen *(extreme lower right)* ties at the wrist.

Like other Egyptians mindful of appearance, the young pharaoh outlined his eyes daily with kohl, a paste of ground malachite mixed with liquid and kept in a container like the double kohl-stick made of wood, glass, and ivory at upper right. Below it is an ivory duck-shaped cosmetic case that swivels open.

Two pairs of sandals and one pair of slippers, all of finely crafted leather decorated with gold, were in the chest at right. Also found was a mittenlike lined linen gauntlet (above) *used for chariot driving.*

The king's name emerging from a blue glass lotus beneath three carnelian sun disks decorates the lid of the mirror case below, shaped like an ankh, the hieroglyph for life. Tomb robbers had stolen the polished pear-shaped silver or gold sheet that served as the reflector.

MOMENTS OF INTIMACY AND LOVE

Affectionate glances pass between Tutankhamen and his only queen, Ankhesenamen, in the ivory inlaid scene on the lid of an elaborately decorated casket from the tomb *(right)*. The smiling, lightly clad queen proffers twin bouquets of lotus flowers to her husband, who bends toward her, his hand raised in greeting. Such delicate scenes of intimacy appear on other artifacts as well.

About four years older than her preadolescent bridegroom, Ankhesenamen, third daughter of Akhenaten and Nefertiti, married Tutankhamen at the time of his coronation. Perhaps she inspired his affection early in the marriage by nurturing him during the difficult transition from boyhood to kingship. And the bonds may have deepened as the couple twice faced the tragedy of a stillborn child.

Later, when her husband's tomb was about to be sealed, the grieving widow apparently placed a remembrance—a wreath of cornflowers—on the golden brow of his second coffin *(below, right)*. Since these flowers bloom from March to April and burial preparations took 70 days, the flowers revealed that Tutankhamen must have perished during the pleasantly cool Egyptian winter.

Mummies of two female fetuses, assumed to be the children of Tutankhamen and Ankhesenamen, were found stored side by side. One child had been five months in gestation; the second may have died in childbirth.

The shroud above, bearing mourners' garlands, covered the second of three coffins. Lifting it, Howard Carter first glimpsed the young pharaoh's face modeled in gold (far right).

THREE MILLENNIA OF GLORY IN THE SUN

EARLY DYNASTIC PERIOD 2920-2575 BC

DJOSER

1ST DYNASTY 2920-2770
2D DYNASTY 2770-2649
3D DYNASTY 2649-2575
Djoser

The roots of Egyptian civilization trail back to around 9000 BC, when rainfall in the Nile region, more abundant than today's, fostered a fertile river valley and savannas to either side. Migrating hunters and gatherers gradually converged along the waterway as the outer lands evolved into the baked sands of the Eastern and Western deserts. By 5000 BC, agriculture had developed and people had settled into villages. Two distinct political regions gradually emerged: Lower Egypt, in the delta, and Upper Egypt, along the river's green corridor. Around 3000 BC, or perhaps even earlier, Upper Egypt conquered its northern neighbor, unifying the nation and giving rise to the First Dynasty. Revered and remote, the pharaohs of this early period were regarded as god-kings. During the Third Dynasty, Djoser (above) erected the Step Pyramid, first of several magnificent monuments to come.

OLD KINGDOM 2575-2134 BC

KHAFRE

4TH DYNASTY 2575-2465
Khufu
Khafre
Menkaure
5TH DYNASTY 2465-2323
Unas
6TH DYNASTY 2323-2150
Pepi I
Pepi II
7TH AND 8TH DYNASTIES 2150-2134

Egyptian culture bloomed during the Fourth Dynasty, a wealthy, stable period that ushered in the country's first great age, the Old Kingdom. The Giza pyramids and the Sphinx—which bears the face of King Khafre (above)—are unparalleled architectural feats of the era; trade and the fine arts flourished as well, and a written language, expressed in hieroglyphs, was now used extensively by the elite. During the Fifth Dynasty, the crown began to lose its aura of authority as the cult of the sun god grew, diluting the pharaohs' power. By the end of the Sixth Dynasty, the nobility had expanded and become independent, and eventually the Old Kingdom disintegrated into rival baronies.

FIRST INTERMEDIATE PERIOD 2134-2040 BC

COWHIDE SHIELD

9TH AND 10TH DYNASTIES
(Herakleopolitan) 2134-2040
11TH DYNASTY
(Theban—before unification of country)
2134-2040

At the beginning of the First Intermediate Period, the pharaohs wielded little power, and civil war and anarchy weakened Egypt. The cowhide shield above was of the type used during the civil wars. Eventually, the 9th and 10th dynasties came to rule all Egypt, but aggressive nobles in Thebes soon declared themselves rightful heirs to the throne, founding their own dynasty. As the separate kingdoms gathered strength, violent clashes broke out frequently along the border between them. During the First Intermediate Period Egypt's cultural development at first declined, then revived.

MIDDLE KINGDOM 2040-1640 BC

NEBHEPETRE MENTUHOTPE

11TH DYNASTY
(after unification of country)
2040-1991
12TH DYNASTY
1991-1783
13TH DYNASTY
1783-1640
14TH DYNASTY
(separate dynasty that ruled contemporaneously with the 13th and 15th dynasties)

The 11th-Dynasty Theban king Nebhepetre Mentuhotpe, reunited Egypt, raising the curtain on the Middle Kingdom. The kings of this period cultivated the loyalty of their centralized bureaucracy, reducing provincial lords to insignificance. They also tended to the needs of the people. Thousands of new acres were converted to use by irrigation, trade was encouraged, and art thrived. Among the gods, Osiris, lord of the afterworld, assumed great importance as his cult expanded attracting rich and poor alike. The cult of the sun god Re continued to be popular.

For more than 3,000 years, the snaking Nile and its splayed delta supported one of the oldest known civilizations, a culture of extraordinary sophistication and maturity. Under the rule of kings of successive—and sometimes simultaneous—dynasties, ancient Egypt vaulted to prominence and maintained its greatness throughout most of its existence. Highlights of its awesome history are presented below, along with names of some of its most outstanding rulers.

SECOND INTERMEDIATE PERIOD 1640-1550 BC

CHARIOT

15TH (Hyksos), 16TH, and 17TH DYNASTIES 1640-1550 BC (In a divided country, kings of these dynasties ruled contemporaneously with one another.)

or unknown reasons, the Middle Kingdom crumbled. Egypt once again slipped into disorder, and the crown of the pharaoh rapidly passed from one king to the next. Meanwhile, the Hyksos from Palestine took over the delta region, founding the 15th Dynasty, which dominated the country for decades. Ultimately, 17th-Dynasty Thebans declared war and, with the help of horse and chariot, a new, lethal piece of military equipment from the Near East (above), liberated the delta from foreign rule, ushering in the New Kingdom.

NEW KINGDOM 1550-1070 BC

TUTANKHAMEN

18TH DYNASTY
1550-1307
Thutmose III
Hatshepsut
Amenhotep III
Akhenaten
Tutankhamen
Horemheb
19TH DYNASTY
1307-1196
Seti I
Ramses II
20TH DYNASTY
1196-1070
Ramses III-XI

Determined never again to allow Egypt to suffer humiliation from outsiders, pharaohs of the New Kingdom strove to build an empire. As loot and captives from the Near East poured into the country, Egypt once again grew wealthy and ever more cosmopolitan, abandoning many of its old ways. The riches found in the tomb of the boy-king Tutankhamen (above) testify to the splendor of the era. A renaissance in painting and in architecture took place, much of the work devoted to Amen, the god of Thebes, whose primacy was briefly challenged during the reign of Akhenaten, the heretic pharaoh.

THIRD INTERMEDIATE PERIOD 1070-712 BC

DOUBLE URAEUS

21ST DYNASTY
1070-945
22D DYNASTY 945-712
(Libyan)
23D DYNASTY
ca. 828-712 (Libyan)
24TH DYNASTY 724-712
25TH DYNASTY
(Nubia and Theban area)
770-712
(Egypt politically fragmented during this period; rival dynasties overlapped)

Invaders from the north and the east wrested Egypt's Palestinian empire from the New Kingdom, while at home the power and prestige of the throne dwindled, the bureaucracy seethed with corruption, and gangs of soldiers terrorized the populace. Eventually Egypt split in two; military men seized authority in Upper Egypt by taking over the priesthood of Amen, while a dynasty of merchant monarchs took control of the delta. Next, dynasties of Libyan descent ruled all of Egypt until they were in turn usurped by the armies of Nubia, a nation to the south. Kings of the new dynasty, the 25th, wore a dual uraeus on their crowns (above) to symbolize the combined rule of Egypt and Nubia.

LATE PERIOD 712-332 BC

NECTANEBO II

25TH DYNASTY
(Nubia and all Egypt)
712-657
26TH DYNASTY 664-525
27TH DYNASTY (Persian)
525-404
28TH DYNASTY 404-399
29TH DYNASTY 399-380
30TH DYNASTY 380-343
Nectanebo II
SECOND PERSIAN
PERIOD 343-332

During the seventh century BC, Assyrians penetrated Egypt, raiding and destroying its great cities. A new Egyptian-based dynasty, the 26th, rose to power in the aftermath, encouraging commerce and the arts during a brief interlude of tranquillity. But in 525 BC, Persians stormed the country's borders, folding Egypt into the Persian Empire and founding the 27th Dynasty. The 28th through the 30th dynasties (which included Nectanebo II, above) included the last independent Egyptian rulers. Then the resurgent Persians destroyed Egyptian independence once and for all. But even mighty Persia was defenseless against Alexander the Great, who conquered the Persian Empire—and Egypt—in 332 BC, signaling the approaching end of the epic civilization.

ACKNOWLEDGMENTS

The editors thank these individuals and institutions for their help in preparing this volume: Guillemette Andreu, Ingénieur d'études au CNRS, Paris; Carol Andrews, Department of Egyptology, British Museum, London; Christophe Barbotin, Département des Antiquités Égyptiennes, Musée du Louvre, Paris; Patrice Bret, Paris; Jacques Chateauminois, Vif (Isère); Eve Cockburn, Detroit, Michigan; Jarrett Cohen, National Center for Supercomputing Applications, Champaign, Illinois; Deanna Cross, Metropolitan Museum of Art, New York; Rosalie David, Manchester Museum, Manchester, U.K.; Christiane Desroches-Noblecourt, Inspecteur Général des Musées Honoraire, Paris; Michel Dewachter, Ingénieur de Recherches au CNRS, Paris; Mary Doherty, Metropolitan Museum of Art, New York; Anna Maria Donadoni Roveri, Museo Egizio, Turin; Guido Fino, Turin; Jean-Claude Golvin, Directeur de Recherches au CNRS, Paris; Zahi A. Hawass, Director General of the Giza Pyramids and Saqqara, Cairo; Marsha Hill, Metropolitan Museum of Art, Egyptian Department, New York; Rosalind Janssen, Petrie Museum, London; Yves Jocteur-Montrozier, Conservateur, Bibliothèques Municipales, Grenoble; Michael Jones, American Research Center, Cairo; Joachim Karig, Ägyptisches Museum SMPK, Berlin; Hannelore Kischkewitz, Ägyptisches Museum, Staatliche Museen zu Berlin; Heidi Klein, Bildarchiv Preussischer Kulturbesitz, Berlin; Rolf Krauss, Ägyptisches Museum SMPK, Berlin; Jean-Philippe Lauer, Paris; David Lawrence, National Center for Supercomputing Applications, Champaign, Illinois; Mark Lehner, Oriental Institute, Chicago, Illinois; Briony Llewellyn, London; Peter Manuelian, Museum of Fine Arts, Egyptian Section, Boston; Vincent J. Murphy, Weston Geophysical Corporation, Westborough, Massachusetts; Charles Newton, Victoria and Albert Museum, London; Diana Patch, Brooklyn, New York; Franz Rutzen, Verlag Philipp von Zabern, Mainz; Bettina Schmitz, Roemer und Pelizaeus Museum, Hildesheim; Elisabetta Valtz, Museo Egizio, Turin; Terence Walz, American Research Center in Egypt, Cairo; Kent R. Weeks, American University in Cairo, Theban Mapping Project, Seattle, Washington; Hag Ahmed Youssef Moustafa, Cairo.

PICTURE CREDITS

The sources for the illustrations in this volume are listed below. Credits from left to right are separated by semicolons, from top to bottom by dashes.

Cover: Jürgen Liepe, Berlin, Egyptian Museum Cairo, background Claus Hansmann, Munich. End paper: Art by Paul Breeden. 6, 7: O. Luz, ZEFA, London. 8: Jon and Anne Abbott. 11: Metropolitan Museum of Art Excavations 1919-1920, Rogers Fund, supplemented by contributions of Edward S. Harkness (2); Metropolitan Museum of Art, neg. #MC 27. 12, 13: Courtesy Trustees of the British Museum, London; Erich Lessing/Culture and Fine Arts Archive, Vienna. 14, 15: Erich Lessing/Culture and Fine Arts Archive, Vienna. 16: Collection particulière, courtesy Bibliothèque Municipale de Grenoble; art by Time-Life Books—Bibliothèque Nationale, Paris. 18, 19: From *The Rape of the Nile* by Brian Fagan, Charles Scribner's Sons, New York, 1975—from *Narrative of the Operations and Recent Discoveries within the Pyramids, Temples, Tombs, and Excavations, in Egypt and Nubia* (Vol. 1) by Giovanni Battista Belzoni, John Murray, London, 1822. 20-24: John Romer, Cortona, Italy. 27: Foto Roemer und Pelizaeus Museum, Hildesheim—Jon and Anne Abbott. 28: From *The Royal Mummies* by G. Elliot Smith, 1912 (Musée du Caire)/courtesy Ashmolean Museum, Oxford. 29: Photography by Egyptian Expedition, Metropolitan Museum of Art, neg. #TAA 1241B. 30, 31: John Romer, Cortona, Italy. 34, 35: Peter Clayton, London/painting by David Roberts. 36, 37: Réunion des Musées Nationaux, Paris. 38, 39: Peter Clayton, London/painting by David Roberts. 40, 41: Painting by David Roberts, courtesy Peter Nahum, London. 42, 43: Peter Clayton, London/painting by David Roberts. 44: Brian Brake/Photo Researchers, New York. 46, 47: Brian Brake/Photo Researchers, New York—Foto Claus Hansmann/Staatliche Sammlung Ägyptischer Kunst, Munich. 49: Reisner Excavation, courtesy Museum of Fine Arts, Boston. 50, 51: Foto Jürgen Liepe, Egyptian Museum, Cairo. 53: Fred J. Maroon. 54: Courtesy Oriental Institute of the University of Chicago; Museum of Fine Arts, Boston. 56, 57: John Ross, Cortona, Italy. 58: Barry Iverson, Cairo, courtesy EAO, Giza. 61: From *The Boat beneath the Pyramid* by Nancy Jenkins, photographs by John Ross, Thames and Hudson, London, 1980/courtesy Hag Ahmed Youssef Moustafa, EAO, Cairo. 62, 63: John Ross, Cortona, Italy (3)—from *The Boat beneath the Pyramid* by Nancy Jenkins, photographs by John Ross, Thames and Hudson, London, 1980/courtesy Hag Ahmed Youssef Moustafa, EAO, Cairo (2)—art by Time-Life Books—from *The Boat beneath the Pyramid* by Nancy Jenkins, photographs by John Ross, Thames and Hudson, London, 1980/courtesy Hag Ahmed Youssef Moustafa, EAO, Cairo (2)—John Ross, Cortona, Italy. 64, 65: From *The Boat beneath the Pyramid* by Nancy Jenkins, photographs by John Ross, Thames and Hudson,

London, 1980/courtesy Hag Ahmed Youssef Moustafa, EAO, Cairo—art by Time-Life Books; John Ross, Cortona, Italy—by Victor R. Boswell, Jr., © National Geographic Society. 67: Courtesy Oriental Institute of the University of Chicago. 69: Museum of Fine Arts, Boston. 70: Susan Dirk/Seattle Art Museum. 73: Fred J. Maroon. 74, 75: By O. Louis Mazzatenta, © National Geographic Society. Art in gold by Fred Holz. 76: Art by Fred Holz. 77: G. Dagli Orti, Paris—Fred J. Maroon—Susan Lapides/Woodfin Camp, N.Y. 78, 79: Fred J. Maroon; art by Fred Holz. 80: Erich Lessing/Culture and Fine Arts Archive, Vienna. 83: Eberhard Thiem, Lotos Film, Kaufbeuren—Jean-Claude Golvin, Paris. 84: Art by Time-Life Books. 85: Brian Brake/Photo Researchers, New York; Jean-Claude Golvin, Paris. 86, 87: Fred J. Maroon. 88, 89: Erich Lessing/Culture and Fine Arts Archive, Vienna; Brian Brake/Photo Researchers, New York. 90: From *Akhenaten: Pharaoh of Egypt—A New Study* by Cyril Aldred, Thames and Hudson, London, 1988. 91: Werner Forman Archive, London. 92: Ägyptisches Museum SMPK, Berlin. 93: Foto Jürgen Liepe, Verlag Philipp von Zabern, Mainz. 94, 95: John Ross, Cortona, Italy—Erich Lessing/Culture and Fine Arts Archive, Vienna. 96: Metropolitan Museum of Art, gift of Norbert Schimmel, 1985 (1985.328.1). 97: Erich Lessing/Culture and Fine Arts Archive, Vienna. 98: Courtesy Trustees of the British Library, London. 99: Foto Jürgen Liepe, Verlag Philipp von Zabern, Mainz. 100, 101: Art by Time-Life Books—Foto M. Büsing/Ägyptisches Museum SMPK, Berlin; Foto Jürgen Liepe, Egyptian Museum Cairo; Eberhard Thiem, Lotos Film, Kaufbeuren; Foto M. Büsing/Ägyptisches Museum SMPK, Berlin. 103: Joachim Willeitner, Rijksmuseum van Oudheden, Leiden. 105: Jon and Anne Abbott. 106, 107: Cliché CEA, Paris from *The Royal Mummies* by G. Elliot Smith, 1912 (Musée du Caire)/courtesy Ashmolean Museum, Oxford; from *The Tombs of Iouiya and Touiya* by Theodore M. Davis et

al., Archibald Constable, London, 1907 (2). 108: From *The Royal Mummies* by G. Elliot Smith, 1912 (Musée du Caire)/courtesy Ashmolean Museum, Oxford; x-ray James E. Harris. 109: Cambridge University Press, courtesy Eve Cockburn (2); James E. Harris—C. Ganet, MCR. 110: From *The Royal Mummies* by G. Elliot Smith, 1912 (Musée du Caire)/courtesy Ashmolean Museum, Oxford; x-ray James E. Harris (2). 111: Foto M. Büsing/Ägyptisches Museum SMPK, Berlin; photography by Egyptian Expedition, Metropolitan Museum of Art (2). 112: Manchester Museum, University of Manchester. 113: Museum of Fine Arts, Boston. 114, 115: From *The Royal Mummies* by G. Elliot Smith, 1912 (Musée du Caire)/courtesy Ashmolean Museum, Oxford. 116: Photography by Egyptian Expedition, Metropolitan Museum of Art, neg. #TAA 55—Foto Jürgen Liepe, Egyptian Museum, Cairo. 118: From *The Complete Tutankhamun* by Nicholas Reeves, Thames and Hudson, New York, 1990. 119: Photography by Egyptian Expedition, Metropolitan Museum of Art, neg. #TAA 812. 121: From *The Complete Tutankhamun* by Nicholas Reeves, Thames and Hudson, New York, 1990, drawing by Ian Bott. 122, 123: Griffith Institute, Oxford. 124: From *Das Ägyptische Museum Kairo* by Peter Riesterer and K. Lambelet, Kümmerly & Frey Geographischer Verlag, Bern, 1975; Griffith Institute, Oxford. 126-128: Lee Boltin. 129: Courtesy Trustees of the British Museum, London—Erich Lessing/Culture and Fine Arts Archive, Vienna—courtesy Trustees of the British Museum—Ashmolean Museum, Oxford. 130, 131: Lee Boltin—photography by Egyptian Expedition, Metropolitan Museum of Art, neg. #TAA 485—photography by Egyptian Expedition, Metropolitan Museum of Art, neg. #TAA 487. 132: Egyptian Museum Cairo—John Ross, Cortona, Italy—Fitzwilliam Museum, Cambridge; Ägyptisches Museum SMPK, Berlin. 133: Andreas Brodbeck, Forsch—G. Dagli Orti/IGDA, Milan, courtesy Museo

Egizio, Turin. 135: Background copied by G. Lovera, courtesy Museo Egizio, Turin; Museo Egizio, Turin. 136, 137: G. Dagli Orti/IGDA, Milan, courtesy Museo Egizio, Turin; Electa, Milan: Istituto Bancario S. Paolo, Turin; Museo Egizio, Turin (2)—G. Dagli Orti/IGDA, Milan, courtesy Museo Egizio, Turin—Museo Egizio, Turin; G. Dagli Orti/IGDA, Milan, courtesy Museo Egizio, Turin (2); Electa, Milan: Istituto Bancario S. Paolo, Turin; Museo Egizio, Turin (2), background Museo Egizio, Turin. 138, 139: Electa, Milan: Istituto Bancario S. Paolo, Turin; Museo Egizio, Turin—Electa, Milan: Istituto Bancario S. Paolo, Turin—Museo Egizio, Turin, background Museo Egizio, Turin. 140: Courtesy Trustees of the British Museum, London. 142, 143: Andreas Brodbeck, Forsch. 144, 145: From *Plates from Researches and Operations in Egypt and Nubia,* 1820, courtesy Peter Clayton. 146, 147: Gaillarde-Francolon/Gamma, Paris. 149: Robert Harding Picture Library, London. 150: Griffith Institute, Oxford (2); Photography by Egyptian Expedition, Metropolitan Museum of Art, neg. #TAA 425; Lee Boltin. 151: Photography by Egyptian Expedition, Metropolitan Museum of Art, neg. #TAA 233—photography by Egyptian Expedition, Metropolitan Museum of Art, neg. #TAA 609; Lee Boltin. 152, 153: Photography by Egyptian Expedition, Metropolitan Museum of Art, neg. #TAA 149—Robert Harding Picture Library, London; photography by Egyptian Expedition, Metropolitan Museum of Art, neg. #TAA 893—photography by Egyptian Expedition, Metropolitan Museum of Art, neg. #TAA 5; Griffith Institute, Oxford; Lee Boltin. 154: Griffith Institute, Oxford; photography by Egyptian Expedition, Metropolitan Museum of Art, neg. #TAA 192. 155: Griffith Institute, Oxford (2); Kodansha, Tokyo, courtesy Egyptian Museum Cairo; photography by Egyptian Expedition, Metropolitan Museum of Art, neg. #TAA 509—photography by Egyptian Expedition, Metropolitan Museum of

Art, neg. #TAA 809; photography by Egyptian Expedition, Metropolitan Museum of Art, neg. #TAA 821. 156: Kodansha, Tokyo, courtesy Egyptian Museum Cairo—Griffith Institute, Oxford; photography by Egyptian Expedition, Metropolitan Museum of Art, neg. #TAA 381; photography by Egyptian Expedition, Metropolitan Museum of Art, neg. #368. 157: Photography by Egyptian Expedition, Metropolitan Museum of Art, neg. #TAA 1350. 158-159: Art by Paul Breeden.

BIBLIOGRAPHY

BOOKS

Aldred, Cyril:
Akhenaten: King of Egypt. London: Thames and Hudson, 1988.
Akhenaten: Pharaoh of Egypt—A New Study. New York: McGraw-Hill, 1968.
Akhenaten and Nefertiti. New York: Brooklyn Museum in association with The Viking Press, 1973.
The Egyptians. London: Thames and Hudson, 1984.

Andrews, Carol. *Egyptian Mummies*. London: British Museum Publications, 1990.

Baines, John, and Jaromír Málek. *Atlas of Ancient Egypt*. New York: Facts On File Publications, 1985.

Belzoni, Giovanni Battista. *Narrative of the Operations and Recent Discoveries within the Pyramids, Temples, Tombs, and Excavations, in Egypt and Nubia* (2 vols.). London: John Murray, 1822.

Bierbrier, Morris. *The Tomb-Builders of the Pharaohs*. New York: Charles Scribner's Sons, 1984.

Bille-De Mot, Eléonore. *The Age of Akhenaten*. New York: McGraw-Hill, 1966.

Borchardt, Ludwig. *Portraits der Königin Nofret-ete aus den Grabungen 1912/13 in Tell El-Amarna*. Leipzig: Hinrichs, 1923.

Breasted, James H. *Ancient Records of Egypt* (Vol. 2). Portland, Ore.: International Specialized Book Services, 1988 (reprint of 1906 edition).

Bucaille, Maurice. *Mummies of the Pharaohs*. Translated by Alastair D. Pannell and Maurice Bucaille. New York: St. Martin's Press, 1990.

Carter, Howard, and A. C. Mace:
The Discovery of the Tomb of Tutankhamen. New York: Dover Publications, 1977.
The Tomb of Tutankhamen (3 vols.). London: Cassell, 1923-1933.

Clayton, Peter A. *The Rediscovery of Ancient Egypt*. New York: Portland House, 1990.

Cockburn, Aidan, and Eve Cockburn (Eds.). *Mummies, Disease, and Ancient Cultures* (abridged ed.). New York: Cambridge University Press, 1984.

Cooney, John D. *Amarna Reliefs from Hermopolis in American Collections*. New York: Brooklyn Museum, 1965.

Cottrell, Leonard. *Lady of the Two Lands: Five Queens of Ancient Egypt*. Indianapolis: Bobbs-Merrill, 1967.

David, A. Rosalie:
The Egyptian Kingdoms. New York: Peter Bedrick Books, 1988.
The Pyramid Builders of Ancient Egypt. London: Routledge & Kegan Paul, 1986.

David, A. Rosalie (Ed.). *Mysteries of the Mummies*. London: Cassell, 1978.

Denon, Vivant. *Travels in Upper and Lower Egypt* (Vol. 1). Translated by Arthur Aikin. New York: Arno Press, 1973 (reprint of 1803 ed.).

Dewatcher, Michel. *Champollion*. N.p. Découvertes Gallimard Archéologie, 1990.

Donadoni, Anna Maria, et al. *Il Museo Egizio di Torino*. Novara, Italy: Istituto Geografico De Agostini, 1988.

Donadoni Roveri, Anna Maria (Ed.). *Egyptian Civilization: Daily Life*. Milan: Electa, 1987.

Drower, Margaret S. *Flinders Petrie*. London: Gollancz, 1985.

Edwards, Amelia B. *A Thousand Miles up the Nile*. Boston: Joseph Knight, 1888.

Edwards, I. E. S. *The Pyramids of Egypt*. Harmondsworth, U.K.: Penguin Books, 1985.

The Egyptian Mummy (University Museum Handbook #1). Philadelphia: University of Pennsylvania Museum, 1980.

Estes, J. Worth. *The Medical Skills of Ancient Egypt*. Canton, Mass.: Science History Publications, 1989.

Fagan, Brian. *The Rape of the Nile*. New York: Charles Scribner's Sons, 1975.

Fakhry, Ahmed:
The Monuments of Snefru at Dahshur. Cairo: Maslahat al-Athar, 1959.
The Pyramids. Chicago: University of Chicago Press, 1961.

Gordon, Cyrus H. *Forgotten Scripts: Their Ongoing Discovery and Decipherment*. New York: Basic Books, 1982.

Goyon, Georges. *Le Secret des Batisseurs des Grandes Pyramides: Keops*. Paris: Édition Pygmalion, 1977.

Goyon, Jean-Claude, and Patrice Josset. *Un Corps pour l'Éternité*. Paris: Éditions Le Léopard d'Or, 1988.

Greener, Leslie. *The Discovery of Egypt*. New York: The Viking Press, 1966.

Hall, Rosalind. *Egyptian Textiles*. Aylesbury, U.K.: Shire Publications, 1986.

Hamilton-Paterson, James, and Carol Andrews. *Mummies: Death and Life in Ancient Egypt*. London: Collins, 1978.

Harris, James E., and Kent R. Weeks. *X-Raying the Pharaohs*.

New York: Charles Scribner's Sons, 1973.

Harris, James E., and Edward F. Wente (Eds.). *An X-Ray Atlas of the Royal Mummies.* Chicago: University of Chicago Press, 1980.

Hart, George. *Ancient Egypt.* New York: Alfred A. Knopf, 1990.

Hawass, Zahi A. *The Pyramids of Ancient Egypt.* Pittsburgh: Carnegie Museum of Natural History, 1990.

Hicks, Jim, and the Editors of Time-Life Books. *The Empire Builders* (Emergence of Man series). New York: Time-Life Books, 1974.

Hobson, Christine. *The World of the Pharaohs.* New York: Thames and Hudson, 1987.

Hornung, Erik. *The Valley of the Kings: Horizon of Eternity.* Translated by David Warburton. New York: Timken Publishers, 1990.

Hoving, Thomas. *Tutankhamun: The Untold Story.* New York: Simon and Schuster, 1978.

James, T. G. H.:
Ancient Egypt: The Land and Its Legacy. London: British Museum Publications, 1988.
Egyptian Painting and Drawing in the British Museum. London: British Museum Publications, 1989.
Excavating in Egypt. Chicago: University of Chicago Press, 1982.
Pharaoh's People: Scenes from Life in Imperial Egypt. Chicago: University of Chicago Press, 1984.

Jenkins, Nancy. *The Boat beneath the Pyramid.* London: Thames and Hudson, 1980.

Kata, Norma J. *Hieroglyphs.* New York: Atheneum, 1981.

Kemp, Barry J. *Ancient Egypt.* New York: Routledge, Chapman & Hall, 1989.

Killen, Geoffrey. *Ancient Egyptian Furniture* (Vol. 1). Warminster, U.K.: Aris & Phillips, 1980.

Kitchen, K. A. *Pharaoh Triumphant: The Life and Times of Ramesses II, King of Egypt.* Warminster, U.K.: Aris & Phillips, 1982.

Landström, Björn. *Ships of the Pharaohs.* New York: Doubleday, 1970.

Lauer, Jean-Philippe. *Saqqara: The Royal Cemetery of Memphis.* London: Thames and Hudson, 1976.

Lehner, Mark. *The Pyramid Tomb of Hetep-heres and the Satellite Pyramid of Khufu.* Mainz am Rhein, Germany: Philipp von Zabern, 1985.

Lepre, J. P. *The Egyptian Pyramids.* Jefferson, N.C.: McFarland, 1990.

Lipke, Paul. *The Royal Ship of Cheops* (BAR International Series 225). Greenwich, Conn.: National Maritime Museum, 1984.

Magi, Giovanna. *Egypt Rediscovered in 19th Century Pictures.* Florence: Casa Editrice Bonechi, 1988.

El Mahdy, Christine. *Mummies, Myth and Magic in Ancient Egypt.* London: Thames and Hudson, 1989.

Martin, Geoffrey T. *The Hidden Tombs of Memphis.* London: Thames and Hudson, 1991.

Mertz, Barbara. *Red Land, Black Land: Daily Life in Ancient Egypt.* New York: Dodd, Mead, 1978.

National Geographic Society. *Ancient Egypt.* Washington, D.C.: National Geographic Society, 1978.

Nightingale, Florence. *Letters from Egypt: A Journey on the Nile, 1849-1850.* London: Barrie & Jenkins, 1987.

O'Connor, David. *A Short History of Ancient Egypt.* Pittsburgh: Carnegie Museum of Natural History, 1990.

Peck, William H. *Egyptian Drawings.* New York: E. P. Dutton, 1978.

Petrie, Flinders. *Seventy Years in Archaeology.* New York: Henry Holt, 1932.

Pope, Maurice. *Story of Decipherment.* London: Thames and Hudson, 1975.

Putnam, James. *Egyptology.* New York: Crescent Books, 1990.

Redford, Donald B. *Akhenaten: The Heretic King.* Princeton, N.J.: Princeton University Press, 1984.

Reeves, Nicholas. *The Complete Tutankhamun.* New York: Thames and Hudson, 1990.

Romer, John. *Valley of the Kings.* New York: Henry Holt, 1981.

Schiaparelli, Ernesto. *Relazione sui Lavori della Missione Archeologica Italiana in Egitto* (Vol. 2). Turin: R. Museo di Antichità, 1927.

Schussler, Karlheinz. *Die Ägyptischen Pyramiden.* N.p. Dumont Buchverlag, 1983.

Simoën, Jean-Claude. *Le Voyage en Égypte.* Paris: Éditions Jean-Claude Lattès, 1989.

Smith, G. Elliot, and Warren R. Dawson. *Egyptian Mummies.* New York: Kegan Paul International, 1991.

Smith, H. S., and Rosalind M. Hall (Eds.). *Ancient Centres of Egyptian Civilization.* London: Kensal Press, 1983.

Spencer, A. J. *Death in Ancient Egypt.* London: Penguin Books, 1988.

Stadelmann, Rainer. *Die Grossen Pyramiden von Giza.* Graz: Akademische Druck—U. Verlagsanstalt, 1990.

Stead, Miriam. *Egyptian Life.* London: British Museum Publications, 1989.

Twain, Mark. *The Innocents Abroad.* New York: New American Library, 1966.

Wilson, Hilary. *Egyptian Food and Drink.* Aylesbury, U.K.: Shire, 1988.

Winlock, Herbert E. *Excavations at Deir el Bahri 1911-1931.* New York: Macmillan, 1942.

PERIODICALS

Aspropoulos, Stavros. "Akhenaten: Hero or Heretic?" *Minerva* (London), May/June 1991.

El-Baz, Farouk. "Finding a Pharaoh's Funeral Bark." *National Geographic,* April 1988.

Brock, Lyla Pinch. "Problems of the Great Sphinx." *KMT,* Fall 1990.

Cox, Christopher. "Ramesses the Great." *The Sun* (Lowell, Mass.), April 24, 1988.

Culliford, Barbara. "New Berth for Solar Bark." *Cairo Today,* July 1982.

Der Manuelian, Peter. "Boston at Giza." *KMT,* Winter 1991.

"Egypt Opens Renovated Giza Tombs to Visitors." *New York Times,* November 4, 1990.

Emery, Walter. "The Tombs of the First Pharaohs." *Scientific American,* July 1957.

"From an Ancient Temple, New Secrets." *Newsweek,* March 6, 1989.

Gore, Rick. "Ramses the Great." *National Geographic,* April 1991.

Hagman, Harvey. "Serendipity in the Sands of Egypt." *Insight,* June 5, 1989.

Hamblin, Dora Jane. "A Unique Approach to Unraveling the Secrets of the Great Pyramids." *Smithsonian,* April 1986.

Iversen, Wesley R. "Today's Technology Unwraps Secrets of Yesterday's Mummified Mysteries." *Supercomputing Review,* January 1991.

KMT, Summer 1991.

KMT, Winter 1990/91.

Lehner, Mark. "Computer Rebuilds the Ancient Sphinx." *National Geographic,* April 1991.

Lemonick, Michael D. "Perilous Times for the Pyramids." *Time,* May 15, 1989.

Maugh, Thomas H. "Scrambling to Save the Sphinx." *Los Angeles Times,* June 4, 1990.

Miller, Peter. "Riddle of the Pyramid Boats." *National Geographic,* April 1988.

Peck, William H. "Miss Benson & Mut: The Short Egyptological Career of Englishwoman Margaret Benson at the Temple of Mut." *KMT,* Spring 1991.

Redford, Donald. "The Akhenaten Temple Project and Karnak Excavations." *Expedition* (University of Pennsylvania), Winter 1979.

Rutherford, John B. "Why Save the Tomb of Rameses II?" *KMT,* Fall 1990.

Smith, Ray Winfield. "Computer Helps Scholars Re-Create an Egyptian Temple." *National Geographic,* November 1970.

Teeter, Emily. "Prince, Priest, Egyptologist Kaemwaset." *KMT,* Winter 1990.

Wilford, John Noble. "At Pyramids, Clues to Laborers' Lot Emerge." *New York Times,* July 11, 1989.

OTHER SOURCES

"The Akhenaten Temple Project Newsletter." No. 1, January 1991.

"Bulletin: Museum of Fine Arts, Boston." Vol. 68, no. 354, 1970.

Hawass, Zahi A. "The Pyramids of Ancient Egypt." Pamphlet. Pittsburgh: Carnegie Museum of Natural History, 1990.

MUSEUMS

Ägyptisches Museum, Munich

Ägyptisches Museum SMPK, Berlin

Ashmolean Museum, Oxford

British Museum, London

Brooklyn Museum, New York

Egyptian Museum Cairo

Fitzwilliam Museum, Cambridge

Griffith Institute, Oxford

Luxor Museum, Luxor

Manchester Museum, England

Metropolitan Museum of Art, New York

Museo Egizio, Turin

Museum of Fine Arts, Boston

Réunion des Musées Nationaux, Paris

Roemer-und Pelizaeus-Museum, Hildesheim

Solar Boat Museum, Giza

University of Pennsylvania Museum, Philadelphia

I N D E X

Egypt, 15, 39
Rosetta stone: 15, 16
Ryan, Donald P.: excavation of tomb KV60, 141

S

Said Pasha: and attempts to preserve Egyptian monuments, 19
Saqqara: necropolis at, 20, 45, 48-49, 68, 70; pyramid at, 66; Step Pyramid at, *46-47*, 50-51, *74-75, 76, 77*
Schiaparelli, Ernesto: excavation of tomb of Kha and Merit, *135*, 139
Scribal equipment: 150
Second Intermediate Period: chariot, *159;* chronology of, 159
Seismic devices: use in archaeological exploration, 148
Sekemre-shedtawy: 21
Senet (game): *139*, 150
Senmut: chief steward to Hatshepsut, 88-89
Seqenenre Tao: mummy of, *114*
Serapeum: excavation of, 68-69
Serapis (deity): 68
Seth (deity): 143, 153
Seti I: *14*, 159; mummy of, 21, 22, 26, *106*, 146; tomb of, 18, *144-145*, 146
Seti II: coffin of, 30
Seven Wonders of the World: and Great Pyramid, 53, 76, 78
Shoucri, Mrs. Asmahan: 84
Siptah: coffin of, 30; mummy of, *108*
Smenkhkare: 102, 105
Smith, Ray Winfield: computerized study of Aten Temple talatat, 83-84
Smyth, Charles Piazzi: 55
Snefru: 55; as builder of Bent Pyramid, 52, 76; as builder of Red Pyramid, 52
Sokar (deity): 48
Sphinx: 20, *34-35*, 45-46, 60, 66; computerized model of, *67*
Steles: 66, 67, *98*, 132, 145
Strabo: on the Serapeum, 68
Sudan: 82
Suez Canal: 19
Suppululiumas (Hittite king): 101, 132-133
Syria: Hittite conquests in, 101

T

Tabes: CAT scan of mummy, *113*
Talatat: 82, 83, 84, *85, 87, 93*
Tell el Amarna: *See* el Amarna

Temples: looting of, 15, 19
Thebes: 10, 20, 21, 81, 100, 114, 119; as religious capital of Egypt, 82, 88, 144; temples at, 83, 88, 89, 90; tombs at, 62, 66, 71, 82
Third Intermediate Period: chronology of, 159; double uraeus crown, *159;* tomb and artifacts from, 23
Thoth (deity): 17, 70, 142
Thousand Miles up the Nile, A (Edwards): 37
Thutmose: hieroglyph cartouche for, *16*, 17
Thutmose I: 88, 110, 134; coffin of, *20;* tomb of, 119
Thutmose II: 88
Thutmose III: 88, 89, 135, 136, 159; mummy of, *23, 25*
Thutmose IV: 13, 86, 136; coffin of, 30; and Sphinx, 60-66, *67;* wall painting from tomb of, *142-143*
Thutmose (sculptor): 98; house and studio of, *100;* and modeled head of Nefertiti, 98, *100;* plaster faces made by, *100-101*
Tia: tombs of, 71
Tiy (queen): 104, 106; and Akhenaten, 85, 86-88, 110; mummy of, *30-31, 110;* sculptured head of, *111;* and Tutankhamen, 126
Tomb KV5: reexcavation of, 146-147
Tomb KV60: reexcavation of, 141
Tomb robbers: 17-18, 20-22, 23, 29, 30, 47, 51, 55, 71, 72, 78, 106, 110, 119, 120, 126, 135, 145, 155
Tombs: ancient Egyptian obsession with, 10; cutaway painting of passageway in, *144-145;* number identification of, 141; reexamination of, 141, 146; restoration work in, *146-147;* typical labor at, 140-142. *See also individual pharaohs*
Tomb workers: daily life of in Deir el Medina, 140-142; strike by, 142; tools and equipment of, *133, 136, 140*
Travels in Egypt and Nubia (Ampère): 40
Tura: limestone quarried from for use in pyramids, 58
Tutankhamen: 30, 70, 71, 72, 143, 145, *159;* accession of, 102; casket of, *156;* clothing and grooming aids of, *154-155;* death of, 104, 149, 156; funeral goods of,

111, 119, 122-124, 126, 127, 128, 130-131, 149-157; gold mask of, *157;* and Horemheb, *103;* as infant sun god Re, *149;* ka figure of, *124;* life and deeds of, 131-132, 149, 150, *152-153,* 156; medical reexamination of remains, 133; mummy of, *29,* 105, 127, 130-131; "mummy's curse" of, 125, 128; and Queen Ankhesenamen, *156;* and Queen Tiy, 126; restoration of old state religion, 102-103, 132, 149; sarcophagus of, 129-130; seals of, 118; throne of, *126;* tomb, diagram of, *121;* tomb of, 10, *116,* 117-119, *121-124,* 131, 134, 148
Tuya: mother of Queen Tiy, 120; mummy of, *107, 110*
Twain, Mark: quoted, 45-46

U

Unas: 158
University of Manchester (England): 112

V

Valley of the Kings: 21, 71; excavations in, 29-32, 117-120; potential finds in, 145-148; reexamination of sites in, 141, 146; village of tomb makers and artisans in (Deir el Medina), 132, *133,* 134, 140-142
Valley of the Kings Resthouse: 148
Valley Temple: 59
Vandalism: ancient graffiti, 34, 46; and pyramids, 52, 73; at site of Akhenaten's palace, 95; and tourism, 73. *See also* Tomb robbers

W

Wadjit (deity): 131
Weeks, Kent R.: excavation of tomb KV5, 146-147
Wilkinson, John Gardner: 92
Winlock, Herbert Eustis: exploration of tomb at Deir el Bahri, 10-14

X

X-rays: use in study of mummies, 105, *108, 110*

Y

Young Memnon (statue of Ramses II): recovery of, 17, *18-19*
Yuya: father of Queen Tiy, 88; mummy of, *107;* tomb of, 120

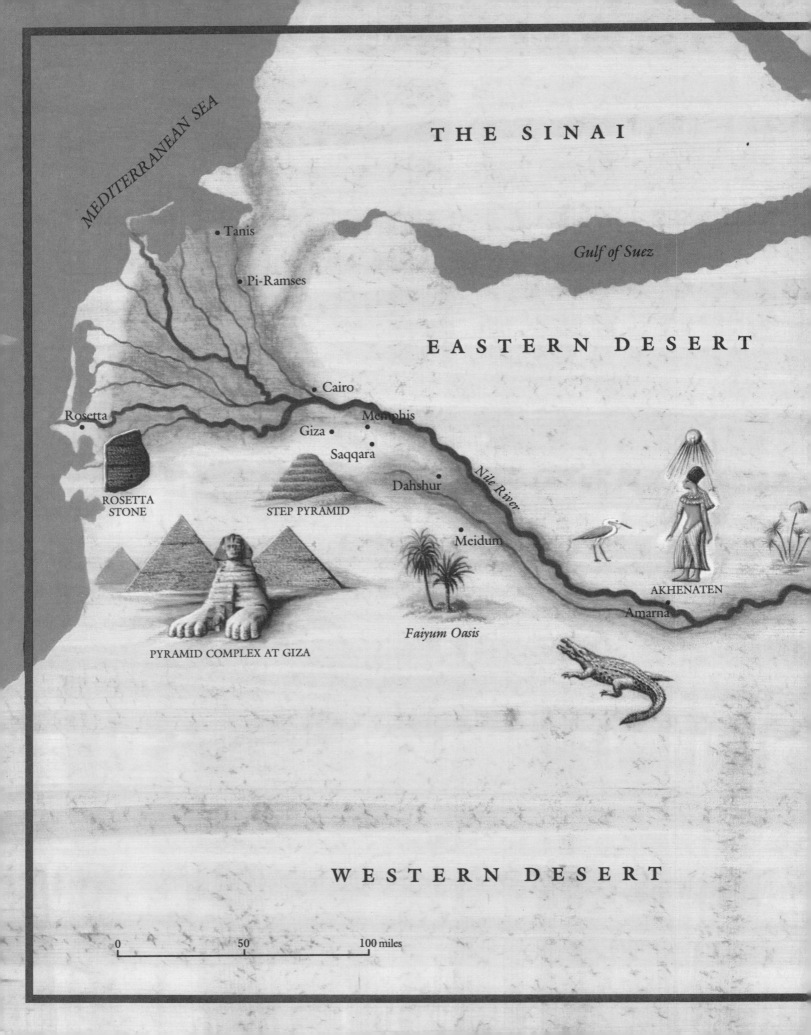

MEDITERRANEAN SEA

THE SINAI

Gulf of Suez

EASTERN DESERT

Tanis

Pi-Ramses

Rosetta

Cairo

Memphis

Giza

Saqqara

ROSETTA
STONE

STEP PYRAMID

Dahshur

Nile River

Meidum

AKHENATEN

PYRAMID COMPLEX AT GIZA

Faiyum Oasis

Amarna

WESTERN DESERT

0   50   100 miles